" *The Homeward Call is a rare gift: a compelling story of grace, deeply earthed, inspiring and provocative in equal measure.* There is an unusual sense here of being offered something more than a memoir. These pages have been lived truly and written prayerfully. Here we have an invitation to walk the ancient paths with a trusted guide on the way that leads us home. "

Pete Greig
Founder of the 24/7 Prayer Movement, Church Planter
Author of *Red Moon Rising* and *Dirty Glory*

" I remember the first time I ever heard Jeff Pratt talk to God. It was in April of 1992. That was the first time I met Jeff and I remember it because I had never heard anyone talk to God like that before. It was as if he was talking to an intimate friend. I remember thinking at the time: "I want to know God like that." I'm forever grateful that Jeff has walked with me on that journey. In a way, it's been a journey home. We have been friends for almost a quarter of a century now and I can say that the words you read in The Homeward Call not only have the potential to be life-changing… they are also authentic. **Jeff lives a life of such deep intimacy with God, it is contagious.** "

Rob Morris
President & Founder of Love146

" In *The Homeward Call*, readers are invited to join Jeff Pratt on a pilgrimage through life and faith. **Deeply personal, yet profoundly universal,** this book offers a path to a rich and fulfilling journey into deeper faithfulness as followers of Christ. "

Jamie Arpin-Ricci
Author of *Vulnerable Faith: Missional Living in the Radical Way of St. Patrick*

" *Homeward Call* is an invitation to follow the often subtle, yet clarion call of faith to discover the essence of life. **Take up this journey and let it surprise you.** "

Stephan Bauman
President & CEO of World Relief
Author of *Possible*

" Jeff Pratt's life story, combined with practical spiritual direction, makes this book on contemplative activism one of my favorites. My faith has been powerfully built up, my view of God expanded, and my desire to see wrongs made right increased exponentially. **This book is a must read.** "

Tom Cole
Director of Hope Grows Farm & Restoration Center
Author of *Pure Heart-Restoration of the Heart Through the Beatitudes*

" It's not a religion it's a relationship', is a phrase used by many of us followers of Jesus but I wonder how many of us actually make it practically so. My friend Jeff Pratt has from the beginning of his journey in Christ, intensely made it an intimate knowing. Every line in this book seemed to draw me and make me hungry for greater closeness. **There is no covering or wrapper on Jeff's very raw, open, transparent presentation of his search and life journey** to be where God created humans to be; walking and talking daily with this personal, loving, accepting and interested-in-each-of-us God. I welcome the invitation to rediscover the somewhat lost slow-dance of meditation, contemplation, pilgrimage, and face to face friendship like Moses and so many others have delighted in over the centuries. "

Dean Sherman
International Bible Teacher
Dean of the College of Christian Ministries
for the University of the Nations
Author of *Love, Sex and Relationships*

" I didn't know Jeff before the invitation to read his book. But now having read it, I feel I know both Jeff and our Lord Jesus even more. **Engaging, story-driven and immediately relevant - this book is ideal for anyone intrigued by the contemplative life or hungry to know Jesus but turned off by religion.** I met Jesus afresh in these pages, and have finished with an invigorated faith, equipped with a toolkit of contemplative practices Jeff so skillfully makes accessible to every reader. "

Andrew Brumme
Producer of *In Pursuit of Silence* film

" All of life is sacred and our journey into eternal life is the journey of discovering our place of origin - GOD. **Jeff is a true pilgrim on this road, an example and exile for Christ in a world of great beauty and pain.** Authenticity, honesty, compassion and wonder hallmark Jeff's call to the deeper life that is ours in Jesus of Nazareth. Onwards and upwards. "

Greg Valerio, MBE
Author of *Making Trouble*
Spiritual Director (FISC) and Founder of
the Society of St. Columba

" Jeff Pratt's story shares his uncommon journey from the Mormon church and into the body of Christian activism through the contemplative practices of the church. **It's an honest exploration, one that gives practical examples of what it means to follow in the way of Jesus.** Take this book. Read it. Savor it. "

Seth Haines
Author of *Coming Clean*

THE HOMEWARD CALL

Zach + Krista,
God's love is yours

12/12/17

Published by AxiomGlobal Press copyright © 2016 by Jeff Pratt

Some name and identifying details have been changed to protect the privacy of individuals.

LCCN: 2016918803
ISBN: 978-0-692-79999-4

Promotional photography by Ian Christmann
Cover design by Marilyn Murray
Book design by jennifer rae design
All illustrations done by Ron Adair except for the drawing of the house, which was done by Noah Cremisino.

THE HOMEWARD CALL

A CONTEMPLATIVE JOURNEY INTO A LOVE THAT WILL NOT LET US GO

JEFF PRATT

Printed by CreateSpace,
An Amazon.com Company

To my Mother who gave me Jesus,
and to my Father who has shown
me what He is like.

" Murphy, all life is figure and ground.
But a wandering to find home. "

-Samuel Beckett, *Murphy*

Table of Contents

Intro

The soothing sound of a trickling rock fountain, and the cool touch of incense-drenched shade drew me into a contemplative garden, outside of Bangkok, Thailand. Here, I had a conversation with an aspiring Buddhist monk in the shadow of a temple that housed the enormous statue of his reclining master. I had just finished sharing the story of Jesus with this young man, when I mentioned that our religions had several similarities.

"Really?" he responded, with a look of surprise.

"We Christians value interior stillness but often don't practice it," I replied. "Our Bible says, 'Be still, and know that I am God.'"

"Do you go to temples to meditate?" he questioned.

"We have church buildings, but we believe God has made His home in us—we are the temples of His Spirit."

"Oh," he gasped in amazement, "If that is the case, you must all take very good care of your bodies!"

"We should," I replied, a bit humbled. We sat in silence for a couple minutes as I wondered where the conversation might go.

"Can you show me how you meditate?" he asked.

Surprised by his directness, I responded, "Sure, I'd love to."

He sat up straight, pulled his shoulders back, and closed his eyes.

"In the Bible, it says, 'In Him we live and move and have our being,'" I explained, "and there are many references to seeking the face of God.[1] First, let's take a moment to clear our minds of restless thoughts and be completely present in the moment."

After waiting for a couple minutes, I said, "Imagine Jesus with the eyes of your heart. I want you to see the Face of Love looking at you."

We waited in silence for about ten minutes. Then I asked, "How was the meditation?"

"I've never had an experience like this before," he said. "I sensed a great gentle power desiring to express Himself to me. He wants me to know how He feels about me." He remained perfectly still, as if awestruck.

"And how does he feel about you?" I asked.

"He loves me," he stammered, "and I'm afraid."

"Why?"

"I think He wants to embrace me." His eyes filled with tears. "I've never been held before."

I was struck by the vulnerability of the statement.

His face lit up as though he'd had an epiphany. "Now I know your mission. You go into the world, listen to your God, and lead people into His waiting embrace. That is what it means to be a Christian."

This book is a return to the central truths of Christianity, truths that are often left unlived. It is an exploration of practices that will not only liberate your heart but will enable you to make Jesus clearly visible to the world. In the pages ahead, we will explore what a life-altering intimacy with God looks like, and through the lens of a Bible-based contemplative spirituality, we will learn to hear the voice of God.

During the Dark Ages, in the medieval town of Assisi, Italy, there were two distinct bells that echoed in the Umbrian countryside. The first bell announced the call to prayer; the second rang in the lepers as they came to draw water. *The two bells symbolize the call to intimacy and prayer and the call to compassionate action on behalf of the marginalized.* Amongst the clamor of this present age—the endless streams of text messages, and the onslaught of social media notifications and advertisements— can we learn to have our spiritual ears attuned to similar, spiritual bells? Such is the life of a contemplative activist, and such was the life of Jesus. It is also the challenge I propose to you as we journey through the pages ahead.

My personal journey of contemplative activism, of learning to hear the calls of intimacy and action, began in the mid-1990s while I was working with Mercy Ships and Youth With A Mission. Over the years, this evolved into leading Silence and Solitude Prayer retreats, compassionate action mission trips and pilgrimages to places like Nepal, Ireland, Italy, Singapore, China and India. Through these travels, an international network of aspiring contemplative activists and mission-minded communities has emerged from over 27 nations. This network has given birth to the Axiom Monastic Community, a community that helps spiritual seekers find their way to God, and trains Christians to answer the plea of Jesus found in John 15:4, *The Message*, "Live in me, make your home in me, as I have made my home in you."

My invitation to you in reading this book is this: *Come and believe in God with me.* If I tell my story, "anything like right," as Frederick Buechner said, "the chances are you will recognize that, in many ways, it is also your story." [2] My hope is that you may learn from my disastrous victories and glorious defeats, and see that I, as Rich Mullins put it from time to time in his concerts, "am just one beggar telling another beggar where to find food." Let's discover what it means to be followers of Jesus whose values match our lifestyles, who love not only the story of God but the One who invites us to live out that story with Him.

This is an open invitation. Will you follow me in the journey and learn how to answer the calls of intimacy and action?

The world awaits God's healing embrace.

"Nothing is more practical than finding God, than falling in love in a quite absolute, final way. What you are in love with, what seizes your imagination will affect everything."

- Father Pedro Arrupe, General Society of Jesus

1

Are Christians True Believers?

"Imagine that there are three people in a room waiting to be interviewed to get into heaven," I said with the quivering voice of a nervous sixteen-year-old. I was a newly ordained priest addressing the Sunday morning Mormon congregation.

"The first person is invited into a room with an interviewer and given one instruction: 'Tell me everything you know about Jesus.' This interviewee unpacks the story, tells the interviewer everything she knows about the life and death of Jesus. The interviewer, in agreement and with hopeful anticipation, nods his head and says, 'This is all true, but is there not one thing you are forgetting?'

'No, I'm sorry. I've told you everything I know about Him,' she replies.

"A look of sorrow and pain crosses the face of the interviewer as the woman is asked to step into the next room."

I paused for effect, then continued. "Another interviewee enters, and is given the same instruction. 'Tell me everything you know about Jesus.' This man is more knowledgeable and quotes all the chronological dates of the important events in Jesus' life. He continues, gives the theological reasons for Jesus' death and resurrection. The interviewer listens intently, and with pleading eyes of deep longing, asks, 'Yes, but is there not one thing you are forgetting?' Perplexed, the man insists, 'No, that's everything.'"

I continued to explain, "Again the face of the interviewer saddens as the man is escorted into the next room.

"The third interviewee steps into the room, and seeing the face of the interviewer, falls to his knees and begins to worship. 'O my Lord! Jesus! How I've longed to see Your face!'" [3]

With the rare but unshakable confidence of a sixteen-year-old, I put down the notes to my message and boldly asked the congregation, "If Jesus Christ were here this morning, would we even recognize Him? We know all about Him, but do we really know Him?" As I looked across the crowd, I awoke to the possibility of a God who longs to be recognized, one who longs to be united with me.

My family was a devout Mormon family, and I was on the fast track to leadership within the Latter-Day Saints Church. Surrounded by a passionate, loving community, and bolstered by several spiritual experiences, I was convinced Mormonism was the only true religion. But this question—*Would I recognize Jesus if he were standing in the room with me?*—awakened a new possibility, one that ultimately sent me on a journey away from Mormonism and into a life-altering intimacy with God.

The Mormon Lifestyle

Years later, I returned to a Mormon Church service in Golden, Colorado, where I had been a member over thirty years ago. I wanted to remember what it felt like to be a member of the community. Orson Pratt and Parley P. Pratt— potential distant relatives, my parents were told— were important early church leaders, so when I was introduced, I received many reverential responses. This was their monthly Fast and Testimony meeting, and one after another, the congregants spontaneously shared testimonies, most of which upheld the Mormon

Church as *The Only True Church*. They became emotional as they shared, and I remembered saying many of the same things in the same place when I was fourteen years old. A wave of nostalgia washed over me, and I found myself thanking God for my Mormon experience. And although I don't believe that every religion leads to God, I do believe that God can use any religion to lead people to Him. In my life he used the lifestyle of Mormonism to prepare me to become a follower of Jesus.

Being raised in a strong Mormon family meant living counter-culturally and with an eternal perspective. Discipline and rules were woven into the rhythm of our days—such was the spiritual training to be a "god" someday—a theology I struggled with even then. Monday nights we had Family Home Evening, and nearly every day we had family prayer. During my high school years, I woke at 5:30 a.m. to attend "seminary." As for rules: alcohol consumption was banned; smoking was banned; sports activities on Sunday were banned; if you were single, slow dancing was banned unless there was a six-inch separation between dancers; and coffee was banned.

However, when Jesus invaded my life when I was twenty years old, and I started attending a Christian church, there was little talk about discipline and rules. Instead, the Church said much about grace—a scandalous grace that transformed my life. But after attending services for two years, I was saddened to see marriages collapse, churches split, and a pervasive instability in the lives of professing believers. I concluded that Mormons were more diligent at living their religious convictions than Christians were at following Jesus as a way of life, and I set out to learn a more devoted Christianity.

What I learned is found in the pages of this book.

Becoming a Follower of Jesus

I've been captivated over the years by how Jesus spent His hours and His days. He was a contemplative activist, one who loved intentional sacred space with his Father, but he also loved being present to poor, the oppressed, and the children. Jesus didn't need to do good things to work His way to becoming a "god" because he already was God. He simply showed us what a life of love looked like.

For a time, I thought myself a true believer because I had faith in Jesus and loved His life. Then I realized, after being involved in full-time ministry for ten years, that true belief motivates us to action.

I became aware of a disturbing reality: I loved the *idea* of a powerful prayer life, solidarity with the poor, and orphan care. But I spent little time actually doing those things. I was in love with a set of ideals more than I was in love with God. I had great values in my life, but few habits and disciplines to match them. *Did I actually believe in God, or was I just in love with the idea of Him?*

There was a call echoing, something drawing me back to a more ancient home-place of Christian belief. I practiced responding to this homeward call, and in the mid-1990s, I began making space for the spiritual disciplines in my life. I had the privilege of getting to know modern-day contemplatives like Brennan Manning, whom I invited to teach in the ministries in which I was involved. I explored the radical discipleship of monasticism and investigated communities yearning for fresh expressions of authentic Christianity, particularly in England. These contemplatives carried similar practices— practices of prayer and service that were not legalistic formulas, but were expressions of an intentional love for Jesus. As Dallas Willard put it, they lived along a "[path] of disciplined grace." [4]

Following this path, I was inspired with a group of friends to start Axiom Monastic Community, a global network of aspiring contemplative activists who have chosen to live by these three "E's"— Encountering Christ, Enriching Cultures, and Emancipating the Oppressed. We began our practice in the Yale University town of New Haven, Connecticut. And early experience confirmed that contemplative activism was the way of Jesus.

Yet in 2005, as the leader of our Axiom Community, I found myself mired in a busy season, a season in which self-importance crept into my life. Concerned I was not living as an authentic follower of Jesus, I cleared my schedule and made space for a weekend of silence, solitude and prayer. After a time of encountering the subtle illusions I had of myself before God, I was sifted into stillness, and a peace into which the world cannot intrude settled in my soul. The inner certainty of being loved by God became my conscious reality.

Following the retreat, refreshed and centered, I flew to Singapore for a speaking engagement at a Youth With A Mission Center. The sights and smells of the city captivated me, but my soul remained placid as a tranquil pool—the fruit of my extended time alone with God. I carried a dozen yellow roses one of the members of the mission center had asked me to pick up for a birthday party later that day. Glancing towards the bus station, a particular woman in the crowd stood out to me.[5] God whispered in the quiet, impressed upon me that I should give the roses to her and say, "These are from your Heavenly Father, from His heart to yours. He wants you to know that He misses you. He is lonely for you. He forgives you and wants you back."

I second guessed the voice of God at first, but then I thought: *What do I have to lose but my pride?* Recalling the words of Brennan Manning, "If you take no risks, you risk not living," I walked to the woman, avoiding direct eye contact with her. I pushed the roses toward her. Taking a deep breath, I fumbled through the words, "These are from your Heavenly Father, from His heart to yours. He wants you to know He misses you. He loves you. He forgives you and He wants you back."

For a moment the woman just stared, bewildered. Then, she burst into tears, and clutched the roses to her chest, sobbing into the petals.

She regained her composure, apologized, and said, "I'm sorry. You need to understand, when I was a little girl, my father was my best friend—my favorite person in the world. We did everything together. He often took me to work with him, gave me rides on his motorcycle, and every year on my birthday he gave me a dozen yellow roses." She paused for a moment, staring at the roses to fight back the tears. Then she whispered, "When I was sixteen years old my father died in a car accident. I became bitter and angry with God; I haven't gone to church since. Now, to my great shame, I'm a prostitute on the streets of this city. I never dreamed that God would forgive me or ever want me back."

At that bus station, with crowds of people bustling by, I watched this humble Thai woman experience her own personal homecoming to God. This divine event led her to discover God's redemptive dream for her life—her activism. Now she leads a home for broken and abused women in Bangkok, Thailand.

Had I not slowed down the pace of my life to attend a personal retreat before arriving to Singapore and given attention to my "To Be" list instead of my "To Do" list, I would never have noticed that woman at the station. Her arms would still ache for the roses her father could no longer give her. Through an act of love, prompted by Jesus, her story was changed forever.

Contemplative Eyes

I am thankful we don't have to pass a tricky interview to get into heaven. We can learn how to recognize and find God now as we acquire contemplative eyes—eyes that are not confined to church one day a week, but search for God in our everyday lives. With these eyes, we'll see opportunities to embody the touch, look, and presence of the Father in a homesick world.

We were made for an ecstatic union with God. Our every spiritual pore, as a thirsty well, yearns for connection with the source of all life and love. When we pause to contemplate, "Be still and know that I am God" (Psalm 46:10), we become aware of the reality that God lives and breathes in us, as He did in Jesus. Divine union, intimacy, and peace are already ours! When we cultivate this realization as a lifestyle, we are practicing what John 15 refers to as "the abiding life," or as Eugene Peterson's *The Message* puts it, we invite the Trinity to make their home in us (John 15:4). And through this kind of living, God affects culture and brings freedom to the enslaved.

Recognizing Jesus for who He is, and achieving this kind of intimacy takes time and, dare I say, work. Work to ask, "Would I know Jesus if He walked into this room?" and to cultivate seeing eyes. Work to follow through with the work the Father shows us. But "[t]rue seeing is the heart of spirituality today," [6] says Richard Rohr. I believe it.

In the last scene of the movie "Gladiator," Maximus's hand glides across the fields of grain, but his eyes are transfixed on his beloved son. It's a beautiful picture of the "homeward call" I believe beckons each one of us—a call toward the home that lies in the center of our being, where the Trinity whispers to us: *You are my beloved, marked by my love, the delight of my life* (Matt. 3:17, The Message). *Come let us make something beautiful of the world.*

That's what this book is about.

Will you become a learner with me and be trained to see with contemplative vision?

Will you join God in making something beautiful of this world, as you turn your heart towards home?

Your Story

Begin the journey of responding to the homeward call of God. Purchase a journal that you can use to process the "Your Story" sections at the end of every chapter.

1. Reflect upon this chapter and make a list of the people and truths/beliefs that you value the most. Review this list and consider how you spent your hours and your days last week. Consider the list and ask yourself: *Do I have habits and disciplines that align with what I value most in life?*

2. St. Francis said, "We only know what we do." [7] Do you really know and believe in the words of Jesus? What adjustments do you want to make as we journey through the book and learn how to follow Jesus as a way of life?

Notes

"*Nothing is more practical than finding God, than falling in love in a quite absolute, final way. What you are in love with, what seizes your imagination will affect everything. It will decide what will get you out of bed in the morning, what you will do with your evening, how to spend your weekends, what you read, what you know, what breaks your heart, and what amazes you with joy and gratitude. Fall in love, stay in love and it will determine everything.*"

- Father Pedro Arrupe[8]

"A Christian is one who points at Christ and says, 'I can't prove a thing, but there's something about his eyes and his voice. There's something about the way he carries his head, his hands, the way he carries his cross-the way he carries me.'" [9]

- Frederick Bueckner, Wishful Thinking

2
"Held by Enchantment" The Early Years

Long before I knew what to call God, and before I started my Mormon training to learn how to become a little god (this is the goal of Mormon spirituality), I felt the presence of love in the world. Somehow I knew that this presence was everywhere yet was very conscious of me. Maybe I felt the echo of "eternity placed in the hearts of all men" (Eccles. 3:11). Or maybe I felt God's presence because I was loved at home. *Home* was the air I breathed—the comforting warmth evoked by the scent of my mother's fresh baked bread topped with butter and honey. *Home* was the calloused, oil-stained hands of my father resting behind my shoulders when a church service went way too long and the baggie of graham crackers ran dry. Home felt like love, and love felt like God.

I loved being raised in a Mormon family of seven kids. Six of us boys came first and little Nicole finished things off. (My parents were determined to keep having children until they got a girl.) But my story begins long before Nicole arrived, with Mom and Dad and the four of us boys, tucked away in upstate New York in a quaint suburb of Binghamton, called Endicott. Gene was my book-devouring, history-obsessed older brother. My younger brother, Steve, was the peaceful, forever trustworthy one. Then there was the blond-haired, blue-eyed newborn named Tim.

In those early years, Steve and I didn't need to talk much. Gene, whom we had nicknamed "the talking machine," filled the air with so many good words there was no room for anyone else's dumb ones. Steve and I learned that our silence made us appear more intelligent. Yet, when we all needed a good giggle, we'd huddle around "Twinkle Toes Tim" and watch his already electric personality shake the crib proclaiming, "touch me, love me, hold me," which we gladly obliged... and haven't stopped doing since.

While Gene was the talker, I was the sleepwalker. I guess I made up for my passive, quiet daytime self by roaming around and causing a ruckus at night. I would get up in the wee morning hours and wander around our single-family home which had been turned into two apartments. One night, I allegedly went into my parents' bedroom, shouted a couple of swear words, and then calmly returned to my bed. On another sleepwalking escapade, I walked into the apartment of the folks above us and climbed into one of their beds. Luckily, it was empty. Imagine the shock the next morning of seeing my upstairs neighbor's inquisitive face peering at me from the open bedroom door!

Meet My Mother

Mom was many wonderful things, but the warm and cuddly, "come sit on my lap" type, she was not. Perhaps this was because her father had raised her alone. I only remember my grandfather as a strong, kindly man who gave us silver dollars and chocolate-covered mints when he visited. As a child, I didn't realize that he'd lost his wife, Jenny, seven months after my mother was born. When my mother was conceived, my grandmother was battling stomach cancer, and the doctors told her she was at great risk because she could not continue preventative treatment. She took the risk, and gave birth to my mother. My grandmother ultimately traded her life for the life of her daughter.

Over the years, I've been overcome with gratefulness. My grandmother loved the life she carried—and the many lives that would follow—more than her own. She took a risk that pointed my family line towards God's redemptive story; He was the ultimate Risk-taker, who also gave Himself away so that we all could have the chance to find our way back home. That is love.

Though my mother was raised by a single father, and without the love of a mother, she always had an ocean of love in her heart for others. Her love welled up in her eyes, and I'll never forget the way she leveled me with one glance. Held in her loving gaze, I felt like I could move mountains.

Meet My Dad

If "home" had a voice, it would have been my dad's. When neighborhood bullies held me hostage, or I sank into a dark nightmare of despair, the comfort and authority of my father's voice was my salvation.

In his younger years, that voice commanded cows, sheep, goats, and a multitude of chickens on my grandparents' farm. And as children, we returned to Dad's blessed homeland, the farm, which was a mere twenty-minute drive from Endicott. It was heaven, a place where, at the behest of my grandfather, our relatives gathered for weekly bonfires near the ancient barn. There we caught fireflies in jars to light our way through the secret forest—a magical, haunted area of woods in the back of the property. Life became a breathtaking wisp of enchantment once I stepped foot on "352 Twining Road."

The farm, and all that happened there, represented my dad better than anything. He was a celebrator and gatherer of people, a fixer of all things broken, and a lover of creation and its creatures. I can't remember anyone who didn't like him. Some people may have been intimidated or threatened by his warmth, his ability to erupt a crowd into laughter. And though my mother had to govern him at times, between her organized and disciplined personality and Dad's love of people and life, they made quite a powerful team.

My Mormon Upbringing

Mom was raised in a Catholic family, and Dad grew up in a Protestant church. Neither wanted to concede to each other's religious beliefs, so when a couple of Mormon missionaries came to the door offering another option (and a family-focused one, at that) they decided it was a fitting compromise. They had already visited many other churches, and none had seemed to welcome them with such open arms as the Church of Jesus Christ of Latter-Day Saints.

At the time, they didn't realize that by joining the Mormon Church, they weren't committing to a style of service but a complex and invigorating way of life. I remember the long hours of Sunday morning and evening meetings, but what stood out more was the hub of community life that revolved around the church facility. There were games and sports in large gyms, dances, and banquets of delicious food. There were also beautiful girls—lots and lots of them! But Mormon events weren't limited to the church building. My favorite was the Monday night "Family Home Evening." It began with a game—perhaps TV or Movie Charades—and ended with a killer dessert.

As far as understanding our religious beliefs and affiliations, I thought we were somehow Mormon and Christian, yet mostly Mormon. We viewed Christianity as only half of the truth, while Mormonism was the completion of it. I saw it as a meatloaf sandwich: Jesus was the "bread of life," but because "man cannot live by bread alone," Mormonism served as the meat of the gospel.

Beyond the outer trappings of the Mormon or Christian churches, our spirituality consisted of an awareness of Someone much larger than any religious organization—Someone who was constant, sometimes subtle, and other times not-so-subtle, backdrop to all good, noble, and beautiful things in the world. Thus, the stand-out events in my early years weren't my Mormon baptism at eight years of age, nor the content of the many services we attended, but the times when God intervened, especially in the life of my father.

Eyes, Ears, and Angels

I remember the spring afternoon when we received the news from Johnson City, New York. Dad was crossing a street when a car struck him in the side of his waist, spinning him like a top through the air. He landed on his feet on the sidewalk he had just left. All the cars and people at the intersection stopped and stared at him in amazement. He looked back at them with equal astonishment. That night at the dinner table, we all sat frozen in wonderment as he told the story.

"I waved the cars on, to get them moving again, which they had a hard time doing after witnessing what looked like a miracle." Then he said a phrase that would follow me throughout my life at needed moments. "God's eyes of love will never leave you—they will follow you always."

A week later, Dad was installing an electrical unit in a department store. While standing on a metal ladder, he connected two cables, assuming that a bare wire that was never used for power would be safe to hold. Suddenly, currents of electricity surged through his body and held him in a rigid death grip. Unable to let go of the cables, he said he tasted metal and brimstone—a sign that life was being taken from him. In desperation, his mind formed the words *My God! I am going to die.*

Mysteriously, the ladder was pushed out from under his feet, sending his body down through the ceiling of the first floor to the main floor of the store, where he landed on his back. Two female employees screamed, holding onto each other in shock. After lying there for a moment, Dad regained movement in his very sore 210-pound body. Then he stood up to walk out of the store, astonished once again by another miracle.

I don't remember if this story was told around the dinner table, but his closing summation of the event became another eternal echo of truth that would revisit me in the years to come: "Call out to God, and He will always hear you. His ears will be attentive to your cry."

Romance and That Gypsy Blood

God's pursuing love—the love that brought us through these events—was the same Presence through which Mom and Dad consistently and passionately cared for us. This created a secure family life, complemented by their 60's love-song-era type of romance, which spanned over fifty years of marriage. I don't think I ever heard Dad call Mom by her given name, Phyllis. He called her by a slew of pet names, the most popular ones being Philly, Precious, Love-bug, and the one word that described how he saw her: Beautiful. And she was beautiful. She had striking dark brown eyes and long hair, enhanced by her poised, tall, stately frame.

Whenever Dad traveled any distance from his beloved, his popular goodbye phrase was, "I will love you forever and a day." And his love for her didn't end with poetic words and affection. To us kids, they seemed like a forever-newlywed couple stuck in time.

While Dad would have been happy building a home on Grandpa's farm for us to live the rest of our lives, Mom was an adventurer who wanted to explore other regions of the States. Prior to living in Endicott, New York, Dad and Mom were married a second time, the Mormon way, in the Salt Lake City Temple. This temple marriage meant they were married *for time and all eternity*, as Mormons say.

In the two years following their temple marriage, we lived in Utah, which is where my younger brothers Steve and Tim were born. Though missing family led us to return to upstate New York, the gypsy travel blood had already entered our veins. We had a yearning to explore more of the Wild West. So, when I was nine years old, we left Endicott and moved to Denver, Colorado, never to return to live in the northeast as a family again.

Though the first decade of my life was not perfect, it was interwoven with the golden threads of a homespun love. As with any true gift, love is only fully appreciated and realized when it is given away. This *giving away* looks different in every life. This was a lesson I learned over 20 years into my story.

Love Full Circle

Years later, I received a startling phone call that sat me down in astonishment. I had just finished a course through the Department of Family Services in Hamden, Connecticut, which I had hoped would license Axiom, the ministry I led, to help needy children.

"I'm sorry sir," the caseworker exclaimed over the phone, "but we can no longer license ministries for foster or adoptive care unless they decide to make legal child care their only function."

I was shocked and disappointed.

"Laws have changed due to abuses of the system. Some organizations have used foster and adoptive care primarily for financial gain. However..." Her tone warmed. "We'd love to personally license you. We have two brothers, ages seven and eight, who've been in foster care for two years, and their foster parents will be retiring this week. The boys may be separated and placed in different temporary homes. If that happens, they most likely will never be adopted because of their ages."

Was she asking me to consider personally adopting two young boys who'd been in foster care for two years, I wondered? I was single, a busy traveler, a leader of a ministry. Although I ached to be committed to someone, I'd always figured a wife would come before children. And in the meantime I was enjoying the freedom of not being married.

"Would you like to meet them?"

"Sure," I said.

We set up a time for me to spend the day with the two boys.

A week later I arrived to the Hamden's Department of Family Services, and the caseworker explained that the boys lived on the streets of Middletown, Connecticut, with their mother for over a year before being placed in foster care. They fled their home due to the fear of physical abuse from their biological father, she said. Then she showed me a photograph of two toddlers at the beach with their father. The older one held his hand while the younger one sat on the man's shoulders, grinning.

She took me to another room and introduced me to Brandon and Patrick. They were wearing clean, crisp clothes, and their hair was perfectly gelled back. They addressed me very politely, "Nice to meet you sir," and both reached forward to shake my hand.

When I asked what they wanted to do on their day with me, they immediately asked if we could go fishing—not surprising, since the caseworker had told me their father had been a fisherman by trade.

On a rocky peninsula at Hammonasset Beach, we breathed in the cool, salty New England spring air as we fished up and down a slippery, moss-covered jetty. The boys caught fish after fish while devouring the famed *Lenny and Joe's* Lobster rolls.

On the drive back to the house, Brandon and Pat sat in the backseat, whispering to each other. Finally, I asked, "Is there something you'd like to ask me?" I waited in anticipation.

"Sir," Patrick said, "we were told by our caseworkers not to ask you this. But my brother and I were wondering... would you consider adopting us? We promise we'll do our chores every day and always stay out of your way."

I was speechless as a wave of sadness enveloped me.

When we returned to my home to get them cleaned up and ready to return to the Department of Family Services, they transformed from being very talkative to quiet and sullen.

As Patrick loaded their backpacks, Brandon came up to me. "Sir, you are high up there, aren't you?"

"I am pretty tall. Six foot three and a half."

"Before you take us back," Brandon asked me with a deep longing in his eyes, "could I come up there?"

As I lifted him onto my shoulders I glanced at our reflection in the large mirror. Brandon was grinning, just like he was in the photo the caseworker showed me.

He leaned down and looked at me, his face inches from mine. "Sir, I don't want you to call me Brandon anymore."

"What do you want me to call you?"

"Can you please call me Son?"

My breath caught in my throat. If this little boy and his brother became my sons, their every joy and pain would affect me for the rest of my life. But in that moment I remembered all the love, joy, and laughter that I had been given in my childhood. So, I looked at him through the eyes of my mother and spoke to him with the voice of my father, saying, "Brandon, today I choose you to be my son. From this day on, you are mine."

"You mean you... you want me?" His brow crinkled in shock.

"My life would be incomplete without loving you."

With a mile long smile he sat up straight, as the deepest joy I ever experienced flooded my soul.

I wonder if we are ever fully part of God's redeeming story until the love we have received in this life has been freely given away? Brandon and Pat offered me that life-altering privilege, the greatest gift of all.

"Loving is its own reward," [10] said St. John of the Cross. Authentic love is love that is not conditioned on how it is received or what its recipient does or doesn't do or become. Authentic love finds its enduring crown in how freely and lavishly it is granted without expecting or needing anything in return.

I am thankful for Brandon and Patrick, my wildly adventurous Irish sons, for giving me the honor of loving them in this life. My heart overflows with gratitude to God for relentlessly pursuing me through the enchantment of my childhood and writing me into the script of His story, before I was born. May I never leave the secure and powerful place upon His shoulders where I can see the world and myself as He dreamed us to be, together with Him.

As we journey through this book, reflecting on our stories, can we give our God the same pleasure of loving us well? Let's allow ourselves time and space for Him to be our Good Shepherd and Guide. Hasn't God chosen to share our every joy and pain, which not only leaves a mark on our hearts but also on His?

"Let the beloved of the Lord rest secure in him, for he shields you all day long, and the one the Lord loves rests between his shoulders."
                                                              -Deuteronomy 33:12

Your Story

Central to the life of a contemplative activist is the awareness that we were loved before the world began. Let's pause and reflect upon God's relentless pursuit of us since the moment he breathed us into being. Let's accept His invitation to the first step of our journey of activism—learning to give away what we have freely received: authentic love.

1. "Before I formed you in the womb, I knew you..." (Jer. 1:5). The word "knew" in this context is one of the most intimate words used in the Bible. This "knowing" is as a husband knows his wife in the intimacy of their physical relationship. Meditate on the following verses, allowing the reality of God's story of you, and its ever-so-intimate beginnings, to capture your heart, as you have captured His:

For you created my inmost being; you knit me together in my mother's womb. I praise you because I am fearfully and wonderfully made; your works are wonderful, I know that full well. My frame was not hidden from you when I was made in the secret place. When I was woven together in the depths of the earth, your eyes saw my unformed body. All the days ordained for me were written in your book before one of them came to be. How precious to me are your thoughts, O God! How vast is the sum of them! Were I to count them, they would out-number the grains of sand. When I awake, I am still with you.

Psalm 139:13-18

2. Sometimes, with sincere hearts, we can love a person for many years with unrealized conditions, hoping that they will be positively influenced by us and appreciate the investment of our time and emotions. This can result in carrying the weight of disappointments and unmet expectations when our hopes are not realized. Is this the case with you? If so, approach God with an open heart, visualizing the person you love. Ask God to show you His way of loving freely as you release the weight and sadness of this situation to Him.

3. Consider God's relentless pursuit of you throughout your childhood and adolescence, though you may not have been aware of Him at the time. After a time of prayerful reflection and thanksgiving, approach God with any worries that may be pressing on your mind today, and slowly read the following Celtic Prayer with an attitude of surrender:

> *"O Father who sought me,*
> *O Son who bought me,*
> *O Spirit who taught me,*[11]
> *I belong to You,*
> *I come to You,*
> *I journey home."*

Notes

"Where a man's wound is, that is where his genius will be."

- Robert Bly Iron Man: A Book About Men

3

Fractures and Fantasies

Most people consider having a speech impediment in pre-school rather cute; this is not the case when you reach elementary school. In fourth grade, on the playground in Lakewood, Colorado, a kid mocked my speech impediment and said to me, "You talk like a baby." A sinking feeling of mortification engulfed me. I couldn't quite pull off the "ch" sound, which came out sounding like "sh" instead. So when I said "chore", it sounded like a place you would walk on next to an ocean. "Chew" would sound like something you wore on your feet.

And if the speech impediment were the only thing, it'd be enough. But I was also a rocker. Not in the cool music way, but in rock in place, back-and-forth kind of way. Most of the time when I was rocking, I wasn't even conscious I was doing it. My second grade teacher, Mrs. Elmer, felt obligated to remind me time and again to sit still. She'd come behind me during a classroom writing assignment and place both of her bony hands on the back of my shoulders, aiming to stop me from my rhythmic, oddly therapeutic swaying. Then, with whiffs of her mentholated cough-drop breath enveloping me, she'd say, "Jeff, you're doing it again. You must stop rocking, and I'm going to be the one to help you quit. You'll thank me twenty years from now." (As an aside, her efforts didn't work. To this day when there are no people around, I will have a good rock and still thoroughly enjoy it; I won, Mrs. Elmer—may you rest in peace.)

In addition to the speech impediment and my habitual rocking, I also lost most of the hearing in my left ear due to a poorly monitored ear infection when I was younger. And did I mention my developing under-bite? These things set the stage for deep insecurities to become part of my life, even though I was raised in a very loving home.

Despite these insecurities, however, I had two gifts that set me apart from most of my peers: I could draw and paint landscapes better than others my age, and when it came to sprinting, I left the competition in the dust. I flew on the wings of the mythical gods Mercury and Hermes—my childhood heroes—when it came to the 50-yard dash in elementary school and the 100-meter sprint in high school. Oh the rush I'd feel when I turned the bend on the racetracks and there were no competitors in my peripheral vision. I won race after race, but still, I knew there would be a day when my best wouldn't be good enough anymore. Someone faster would eventually come along, and when that day came, what would I be known for? My inadequacies?

Teenage Wonder and Angst

The summer I turned fourteen, a wonder of wonders happened— I jumped to my current height of six feet and three-and-a-half inches. Yes, I thought, *There is a God and he's showing mercy to this quiet rocker-runner, after all!* I went from being a short, thin, rather peaceful and relatively unnoticeable child, to a tall, gangly, rather peaceful and relatively unnoticeable teenager. Uncomfortable with my sudden height and resulting poor posture, my head would often arrive places before I did. That's where Mom came in. Kindly but directly, she'd have me stand with my back and shoulders straight against the wall. She'd ask me to step forward and walk with my shoulders tall and straight.

Wow, I thought, already feeling too tall. *Look at me now, towering above the world.*

I was learning to walk in a way I didn't feel inside, insecure as I was.

Like most teenagers, I was a paradox of securities and insecurities. I was very secure in my faith because I lived with the certainty that Mormonism was the only true religion in the world. But though I was secure in my beliefs and my parents created a secure home life, I was insecure about everything else. So, like many teenagers, I retreated to daydreaming and living in fantasy worlds. Why should I endure the downward, condescending glances thrown up at me from others when I could get lost in books, in stories, in the conquest of kingdoms and the love of exotic princesses of Earthsea, Narnia, and Arthurian England? Often, my schoolteachers caught me staring out the window and ushered me back to reality.

"Jeff we're losing you," they'd say. "Come back to us. What's so exciting out there?"

If you only knew, I thought, with a secretive grin. I knew I was made for far loftier pursuits than mere Algebra 1, which I was taking for the second time.

Secure Mormon Foundations?

The Mormon lifestyle was difficult in my school years. It wasn't cool to be forbidden to drink Coke. And while other teens were dabbling with sneaking a toke of Marijuana behind the restroom or bleachers, I felt guilty for taking a sip of coffee. Holiness was a moral code, a list of dos and don'ts that I adhered to so that I might "eternally progress" toward perfection. In many ways, I felt a higher standard of holiness, conduct and discipline than Christians. We woke at 5:30 in the morning and attended Seminary classes before our first class in high school. We abstained from all vices. We were pure. We were trained to live for *eternity*, to want something more than gratification in the now.

I lived with an inescapable sense that there was a noble call and purpose to my life, despite my out-of-date Beatles' haircut and my lanky frame. Mormonism cultivated this inner sense of security and destiny. In Sunday school we sang, "I hope they call me on a mission, when I have grown a foot or two." I lived in the excitement of knowing that, in my late teen years, I might be called to another country to share the good news about "the only true church on the face of the earth." And I knew this corresponding truth—once I returned from my mission, I would have my pick from a batch of breathtaking young Mormon ladies. Simply put, a returning Mormon missionary didn't need to be *that* good-looking to win one of the ladies over. And being married to a returned missionary, the lucky bride would have a secure future as a goddess in eternity. This being the case, even I could score big time after I returned from a mission.

A Mormon's sense of mission, family, and community was an invisible net holding everything together, perhaps even more so than Mormon doctrines and practices. And it wasn't that doctrines and practices didn't exist. But the rules were assumed truths you acted on because they were expected of you. The practices became habitual; they were the only way to eventually reach the highest heaven, the Celestial Kingdom, where you would someday reign with your future wife.

Eventually, there came that part of my growing-up years where a combination of my parents' oh-so-appealing romanticism and a good dose of hormones led me to try out some of my more chivalrous fantasies and find the first great love of my life. Church outings, early morning seminary, and my French class became my new hunting ground. Though I continually fell into extreme infatuations with girls who never knew I existed, I was no emotional prostitute. I was that hopelessly devoted fellow who loved a girl for at least six months, maybe even a year or longer. The way I saw it, since my dad had married my Mom at 18 and they began having children by 19, I had only 4 short years to find the one I was going to spend "time and all eternity with." She would be my future goddess.

I wanted to have a head start in life, so I gave away my first ring when I was only 14. Her name was Christine, a stunning Hispanic girl with long black hair that, of course, tumbled down to her waist. She was poised and elegant, and though her stature was small, she carried a shocking sense of confidence. A hush passed over the boys' section of Sunday school whenever she entered. I knew I needed to do something quick, or she would be taken from me. So, I spent my hard-earned money on a ring from Target. I was sure that its beauty and my devotion would seal the deal. Instead, it was returned to me immediately through her parents to my parents. This was, of course, an embarrassment that didn't help my insecurity. What went wrong?

While I was hacking through the weeds and wilds of adolescence, Mom and Dad decided that four kids were not enough. So, after a five-year gap, they started another run of children, which we older siblings referred to as "The Dream Team." Reid and Lee were born in Colorado. Nicole was born in California. And as the Dream Team grew, it became apparent that they were just better kids than us: more innocent, more compliant, and less troublesome. I guess Mom and Dad finally had parenting down to a science by the time the Dream Team came around. And though I loved the addition of new siblings, it wasn't cool to have younger siblings when I was in my mid-teens.

An Emotional God?

The truth is, I was emotionally awkward in my childhood and teen years—a stilted hugger, wooden in the ways I showed emotion. I was like my mom in that way. Dad was affectionate in how he demonstrated his love, but receiving and giving affection didn't come naturally for Mother. Later, I learned that my mother endured very real hurt, hurt that haunted her and caused her to carry an unwarranted sense of guilt and an inability to fully accept she was worth loving. The details are not mine to share, but her guilt and shame were real.

Even without knowing Mom's story, I think some of us kids took on different shades of her tendencies toward guilt and unworthiness. Also, the culture of perfectionism and moralizing of Mormonism actually exacerbated those tendencies. When you are working your way to godhood, you have little time for imperfections or the acknowledgment of your emotions. Imperfections and emotions are what you were trained to hide.

And even though my father loved me fiercely, he rarely showed other emotions. The only time I ever saw my dad almost cry was at a family prayer time shortly after Grandpa died. I concluded that men lived beyond their feelings. Thus, I was confused by the biblical texts revealing the God of strong feelings, one who responded out of deep emotion. The New Testament text of Jesus throwing over the tables of the moneychangers was utterly shocking to me. It always got me thinking: *Didn't Jesus lose control of His emotions there for a moment? And isn't He supposed to be the Son of God, the King of Kings?*

Our Overlapping Stories

Sometimes I wonder if we arrive in this world whole and integrated, but then we encounter the shadowed side of humanity that causes us to ponder the possibility that maybe we don't belong here after all. For those of us who felt loved in our younger years, we may react to this realization with the question: Is this world the home I thought it was in the magic of my childhood?

Aren't we all a combination of securities and insecurities, the product of the good and bad parts of those who raised us? What made them who they are is a strong informer of who we are. With the added script of our own fractures, sometimes the result can be toxic. We need a greater story, a higher all-encompassing love that our childhood and adolescence yearnings could only reflect. We need a story that unites, redeems, and gives understanding to our own narrative.

Looking back, I remember one of the very first moments when this redeeming love became a reality for me personally. I was leading a Youth With a Mission Discipleship Training School in east Texas in my early thirties. The school was being held at "Last Days Ministries," a ministry started by Keith and Melody Green. I was enjoying an ever-growing relationship with God, but emotionally my heart wasn't fully alive. I couldn't even remember the last time I cried. But that would change late one night.

A knock came on my mobile home trailer door. A British couple in their mid-thirties stood staring soberly at me.[12]

"What's going on?" I asked, sensing something was seriously wrong.

"Jeff," Mark said, without small talk, "I'm struggling with suicidal thoughts. I need to give you my handgun so I won't be tempted to use it." He passed a small pistol to me. I asked the origins of his suicidal thoughts, and he continued.

"When I was five years old, my Father put me on top of a wall," Mark explained. "He stood at the bottom, stretched out his arms to me and said, 'I love you son, jump to me.' So I jumped, but he stepped away. My body hit the ground and so did my heart. He was my hero. When I came down hard he said, 'Son I know this hurts now, but this will teach you a very important lesson: No one is worthy of your trust, especially not leaders or God. Everyone is imperfect and will eventually disappoint you. Close down your heart now. Don't allow yourself to feel anything anymore and you'll be protected from all hurts, wounds and pain.' So, I listened to my father and did exactly as he said. I've never felt hurt from that moment on. But here is the problem: I also haven't felt love. Our marriage isn't working." He glanced at Michelle, "I know I can't trust her, and I can't feel her love for me. That's how it is."

Mark's story clarified what I'd observed in him during the two months of their attendance in our school. Never had I seen a flicker of emotion cross his face. That night I got down on my knees and prayed. I pleaded with God that he would reveal his heart and healing to Mark and his wife Michelle.

The next morning, we gathered to hear a speaker with quite the reputation for being a crazy Charismatic woman. She had a ministry some called prophetic, while others believed it to be out-of-the-box and unpredictable. I was suspicious and skeptical as she started her first teaching session with a series of jokes that didn't impress me much. But the next thing I knew, while the group was still laughing at her latest joke, she zoomed in on Mark and his wife Michelle, who were sitting in the front row of the class. She abruptly got serious.

"Excuse me, sir," she said, "but why are you laughing when inside your heart is breaking? Why are you laughing when last night you were contemplating suicide?"

The atmosphere in the room grew tense as the laughter turned to alarm.

Staring with utter confidence into Mark's eyes, Jill continued with profound assurance: "Today, God, your Father, wants you to know that he stands at the bottom of the wall of your life. With his arms outstretched to you, he says, 'I love you my son, and I want you to jump to me. I will catch you. I will never let you go. Jump son, jump. I am worthy of your ruthless trust.'"

At that moment, Mark crumpled to his knees and for the first time in years began to weep. Michelle followed him, leaning her head against his. Then immediately, as if someone else were leading me, I walked over to Mark and did something that was very uncharacteristic of me. I knelt down in front of him, enveloped him in my arms, and hugged him, feeling warm tears rolling down my cheeks. I was overwhelmed with the sense that God, who had missed the emotionally engaged presence of his son for years, was now welcoming him home. Mark's heart was healed that day—so was God's, as well as mine. The table of my repressed emotions had been violently overturned. No longer was I a by-product of both the good and bad events that I had experienced in my life, but I was becoming a character in a far greater story. The stilted hugger of my past found redemption's road, and my once detached soul found its oh-so-passionate King.

Your Story

I believe we arrive into this world whole and integrated, but then we encounter the shadowed side of humanity. The fractures (hurts and wounds) that we incur during this encounter can either rob us of the knowledge of who we were born to be, or they can serve as a spiritual director and lead us into a deeper union with God. Let's determine which is the case in your story as I guide you through some reflective exercises, giving time and space for God to lead you to redemption's road.

1. Which statements below are common thought-patterns for you?

I am not allowed to make mistakes.

I must be approved by certain people to be okay.

I am valuable based on my intelligence, wealth, and what I do instead of for who I am.

Other people's thoughts and feelings are more important than mine.

I am not complete; therefore, I do not have the right to assert myself.

2. Do you hold yourself in high regard despite your limits and imperfections?[13] In considering our fractures and/or weaknesses, meditate on the following scripture passage. Wait and listen to hear God's *still small voice* and see if there is any truth, or perspective He wants to share with you.

> But he said to me, 'My grace is sufficient for you, for my power is made perfect in weakness.' Therefore I will boast all the more gladly about my weaknesses, so that Christ's power may rest on me. That is why, for Christ's sake, I delight in weaknesses, in insults, in hardships, in persecutions, in difficulties. For when I am weak, then I am strong.

> 2 Corinthians 12:9-10

3. While considering your upbringing, reflect on these questions:

How are you a combination of both the good and bad parts of the stories of those who have raised you?

What part of you is in need of finding redemption's road?

4. Let us pray together:

O Lord, search me and know me. My past is a deep aching abyss of darkness and light, a poorly tended thirsty well that sometimes offers me refreshing springs of memories as a good teacher. At other times it is a tormentor that withholds its healing waters because of my consistent failures. So I come to you, Gentle Healer and Gracious Forgiver. Teach me to have compassion on myself. How can I give to others what I have not first received from you? If your power is made perfect in my weakness, then I should start rejoicing that I have them, and stop seeing my story as outside of yours.

Notes

" Where a man's wound is, that is where his genius will be. "

- Robert Bly [14]

"To pursue a vocation in any field without the perspective of the world's poor—where God's heart and good news is centered, is folly."

- *Craig Greenfield, Director of Alongsiders International*

4

Inner and Outer Poverty

After living in Denver for five years, our family ventured out and moved farther west to explore new frontiers, having no final destination in mind. We were intrigued with northern California, and as we contemplated the move, I was excited. I would have an opportunity to reinvent myself.

Since I didn't find "The One" in Colorado, I was sure a better version of myself could find her on the balmy sun-kissed shores of Cali. So with a new modern hairdo and stylish threads, which of course erased years of insecurities, I entered a new Mormon congregation in Santa Rosa, all psyched for new friendships and fresh female possibilities. However, I dreaded the Sunday morning introduction we would endure in the new "ward" (the Mormon term for a specific church congregation) in which we sought membership. My brothers and I had each been given Dad's name for our middle names, which meant the facilitator of the service would announce us as follows: "We would like to welcome Arthur George Pratt and Phyllis Ellen Pratt to our ward as well as their children; Gene Arthur Pratt, Jeffrey Arthur Pratt, Stephen Arthur Pratt...." By the time it got to Tim everyone would be chuckling. It all seemed very uncool and embarrassing, and I only had one chance to leave a first impression. I should've just rolled with it and laughed, but no, I took it all too seriously.

The Sunday service came and went just as I'd imagined. Little did we know at the time, but that awkward introduction was the beginning of the Pratt brothers not only being introduced to congregations, but being asked to sing for them, too. We loved music as a family, and Mom quickly pointed out that our singing voices sounded good together.

Personally I loved the thought of singing, and Mormonism, being a very cultured religion, gave many opportunities to develop personal gifts and aspirations, especially in the field of the fine arts. Also being that our last name was Pratt, and Orson and Parley P. Pratt were some of the early church leaders, many thought we carried a kind of legacy. So on occasion, we sang as a family, mostly as brothers at church services and occasional events. Though I deeply enjoyed singing solo in my confident moments, I thought it was uncool to sing together with my brothers, especially in harmony, which is how we began. Mom became our catalyst and motivator. I can see now that even more than seeing potential in us as a singing team, Mom's yearning was always to push us, and others, towards a higher way of living and loving. She saw our singing as a vehicle that could be used to inspire and challenge the church to rise up and accept its true calling to love God and others well. In that way she was one of the most prophetic people I ever knew.

Our professional musical trainer, who taught us our first three-part harmony musical piece, was Brother Hicks, the man who coached The Osmonds—then famous TV performers—when they started off as a barbershop quartet. The song was called, "Jesus the Very Thought of Thee." Though tonally our voices blended well as brothers, it was often the truths of what we sang about that had the greatest impact on others. Usually the truths had something to do with the life, death and resurrection of Jesus, which fit Mormon theology. The resurrection was a truth we believed; it just wasn't the complete truth. Jesus was only the bread in the meatloaf sandwich.

My False Self and Aslan

While we trained with Brother Hicks, and as I was starting personal voice lessons, my confidence in my ability to perform live grew. Four years prior, in a speech therapist's office in Denver, I found my *ch*. Braces had also straightened my crooked teeth and under bite. I began to fill-out, and girls started taking notice. These external changes still didn't change my internal fractures and insecurities, though; they were very much alive.

Hoping to whitewash my insecurities, I reminded myself that I was growing into a man and would be a god someday. I decided I wouldn't be that wimpy person who hurts anymore, or is hurt-able. Instead, I'd prove I was worth love and respect, that I had it all together. I allowed the emergence of the beginning of what is often called, a *false self*, a term used to describe the identities we create to validate us in the eyes of the world. As the Christian mystic, Thomas Merton said, "Each of us is shadowed by an illusionary person, a false self. This is the man I want to be but who cannot exist because God doesn't know anything about him. And to be unknown by God is all too much privacy."[15] The good artist, the fast sprinter, the singer in training, the put-together person—these were my false selves.

Those parts of me that wouldn't fit into one of my self-centered identities, those I didn't like, I stuffed away into the shadows of denial. No longer was I going to show sensitivity or expose need, which is the very incubator for the intimacy I needed. I did not want people to know that all I wanted was to be accepted and admired. And when I didn't feel this affirmation, I would often sexualize the need for intimacy in my mind. I didn't feel secure enough to risk genuine connection with a girl my age, so I either fantasized a life with any given girl, or resorted to the quick fix of lustful thoughts. This became a heavy weight in my life because I held the position of "teacher" at church and didn't feel like I was living up to the moral standard that this Mormon office required.

Co-existing with these struggles was a haunting from another world. Though my inner fantasy world of chivalry and knighthood was quickly fading, Aslan, the Lion from Narnia, the type and shadow of God, would not go away. I told him I was too old for him now; I didn't need him or the other animals now that I was getting pretty good with real people. But he didn't listen to me. Aslan was everything my heart imagined Jesus to be, and I knew no one could outgrow Jesus; you just want more of Him.

Emerging Light

Before moving to Santa Rosa, California, we lived an hour north (though only for a short time) in a more rural setting. Due to the uncertainty of Dad's work, all eight of us had the adventure of camping for over four months alongside Mendocino Lake. Most families our size would consider camping a month together a stretch, but not us. We had a mini-motor home that slept eight, and to make living easier on us, Gene and I slept in a tent we put up on the same camping site. We so enjoyed the simple life, with fewer chores and more s'mores! Those golden dry hills surrounding the drought-thirsty lake became a backdrop for significant spiritual realities that affected the direction of our lives forever.

Family Home Evening nights took an earthy, simpler tone while camping became our new life for a while. Mom picked up Catherine Marshall's book, *Beyond Ourselves*, and read a couple of chapters to us every Monday night. One of those evenings, as we sat in collapsible chairs around the empty fireplace, Mom began, "We've been talking about what it means to be a true Christian and have an ever-growing relationship with God. Marshall mentions that becoming a Christian involves surrendering your entire life to God. However, she says, we don't begin there because we haven't yet learned how to trust Him."

She continued, glanced up, drew our eyes in, and continued.

"She suggests we start by surrendering one of our problems to God. As we give Him a problem, and leave it with Him, we will see how both the issue and our own hearts begin to change. This prepares you," Mom said, "to learn how to trust God more so that you can eventually give Him all of your life, not just part of it."

"Jesus wants everything," she explained with heartfelt passion. "He died for the redemption of every part of us. Yet He knows that we don't know Him in a personal way yet, so tonight let's start the journey of trust by giving Him one of our problems. Let's watch and see what He will do with it this week, and next Monday night we will talk about it." I was so excited about this exercise. This sounded like such a natural and relational way to approach God; however, I felt guilty about my struggle with sexual thoughts, which made me feel unworthy to hold the office of a teacher at church. How could people worship me as a god someday if I harbored secrets like this? That evening I went alongside the lake, and as the gentle waves lapped at my feet, I shared my issue, and other parts of my heart, imagining Aslan as Jesus. I felt confident He heard me, as my father said years ago; "Call out to God and He will always hear you. His ears will be attentive to your cry."

Our next family home evening was very profound as we shared what God had done with our individual problems. The power of my temptation to sexualize my need for genuine connection lessened as I started to believe in more of a relational God who seemed to desire a greater intimacy with me. Alongside this spiritual awakening, Mom was also struck with the awareness that God was equally interested in how we translated His compassion to those in need. Up to that point I assumed that what was most important to God was anything involving our personal interaction with Him: prayer, Scripture, or partaking in the sacrament. I thought our service to Him was of lesser importance. My paradigm was about to change.

A few days after that night of study, Mom was reading a book in a park in Ukiah when she noticed a Native American, one who looked homeless, sitting under a large oak tree. The only food she had in the car was a banana so she walked up to the man and gave it to him. He gladly received it with a warm nod. She noticed he was holding something in his hands, and his head was downcast as he caressed his native headband. Mom gently took it from him and tied it around the crown of his head. Her hands were shaking from being a bit nervous and because she felt strongly about the words that she was going to say to him. "You are royalty," she said. "You can walk with your head held high; you were created to be a son of God."

He immediately stood up straight, as if being summoned by his chief and said, "You are right. I have forgotten who I was made to be. Thank you!"

"The Least of These"

That Christmas, we continued a Pratt family tradition. The kids put together a special Christmas Eve program, reenacting the nativity passage. Mom then read a long Helen Steiner Rice poem, "The Christmas Guest." I don't remember actually listening to it or understanding its meaning, until our holiday season in Ukiah. But that Christmas Eve, as mother's eyes teared up while reading the last couple of stanzas of the poem, the message captured me and made Mom's simple act with the Native American seem so profound.

The poem tells the story of a man named Conrad whose family had long passed away, leaving him alone on another Christmas day. To his great joy one night he had a dream, in which Jesus told him, "I'm going to be your Christmas Guest." With much excitement Conrad prepared his home for his most Divine visitor. Christmas morning arrived and he heard a sound outside. He ran to the door expecting to see Jesus, only to find a poor beggar. Having compassion on the man, he invited him in and gave him warm shoes and a coat to wear before he journeyed back out into the snow.

"Thank you so much for the wonderful Christmas gifts!"

"A Merry Christmas to you," Conrad replied.

At Midday another knock came to his door. Again Conrad jumped to his feet in excitement and ran to the porch only to find an older woman who needed a place to rest. He invited her in, sat her by the fire, and gave her some tea and food to eat.

A third time, Conrad heard another sound outside his door, but this time it was a child lost in the night whom he comforted and helped find her way home. In sadness Conrad retired to his bed, lifted up his voice, and asked God, "What kept you from coming to call on me, for I wanted so much for your face to see?" Soft in the silence a voice he heard,

"Lift up your head for I kept my word -

Three times my shadow passed your floor,
Three times I came to your lonely door.

For I was the beggar with the bruised, cold feet,
I was the woman you gave to eat,
And I was the child on the homeless street.

Three times I knocked and three times I came, and
Each time I found the warmth of a friend.

Of all the gifts, love is the best,
And I was honored to be your Christmas Guest." [16]

The poem echoed the words of Jesus, "as much as you have done it to the least of these my brethren you have done it unto me" (Matt. 25:40).

In hearing this story I was awakened to the reality that contemplation isn't limited to scripture and prayer practices, but it's self-forgetful service that brings comfort to the very heart of God. I remembered how my mom didn't allow her insecurities, her false self, to keep her from approaching the Native American in the park. I wondered, could I also lose myself and let go of my self-centered identities long enough to learn how to love?

Years later this poem would continue to impact me. While on a spiritual retreat in Bournemouth, on the south coast of England I journeyed past the chalk white cliffs near Old Harry's Rock and into the well-worn peaceful trails that hugged the coastline. I held an expectation that the Lord somehow wanted to make Himself known to me in a special way as I made this space and time for Him to fill.

After hours of silent wanderings, praying and reading scripture, my heart still felt restless. I sensed there was a unique way God wanted to give Himself to me and that I needed to stop seeking to encounter Him using my usual methods. I felt even in the beauty of my surroundings I was still striving to make something happen, and I was also hungry—not a good combination. I strolled into the old town of Swanage to find food. While I sat on a low stonewall adjacent to the old town center considering my options— fish and chips, or a turkey meat pie—I noticed an old, very weathered man shuffling down the cobblestone lane. His wardrobe was tattered, pieces of it dragging on the ground as he walked. A brown knapsack was flung over his shoulder as he held a large brown paper bag with the outline of what looked like an overripe piece of fruit bleeding through.

I watched, then shifted my gaze when I saw him turn and begin to walk toward me. *He's coming to beg*, I thought, wondering if I had any British sterling in my pocket. I waited as he approached, but he didn't lift his palm and didn't ask for money. He kept coming toward me with small shuffles until he invaded my personal space to the point where I could smell the musty sea salt of his outer robe. He stopped when he couldn't go any further without toppling me over backwards.

Then in slow motion he leaned his head against mine and simply stayed there. I was paralyzed. What was he doing? We stayed there for a minute or so, and oddly enough, the awkwardness of the encounter completely melted away. My false self, the self that always cared about what other people thought, was diminished. I experienced the man and the presence of the Divine. I felt his sadness and his companionship. I felt loved. I felt Jesus as I leaned against his mane. We never exchanged a word, and a few moments later, he lifted his head and slowly walked away. Even still, he has never entirely left me.

I encountered the crucified Christ that day in what Mother Teresa calls, "the distressing disguise of the poor." I discovered that the more I enter into a loving union with another person—even for the shortest of times—the more I become my true self, a person who was made to love. From that moment on I was awakened to the reality of this vulnerable place where our Jesus can be found and where his homeward call can be heard.

Waiting in Hope

I have a friend named Grant who serves as an undercover detective in brothels in northern Thailand. It's the most difficult job of his career because of the many children he is unable to help due to political corruption. There was one such girl named Sarah, whom he befriended and had the joy of leading into a relationship with God. Sarah was twelve years old, very soft-spoken, and loved to make Grant her special noodle soup for lunch. She was an artist and brought him pictures of the heaven she imagined. In the mornings he noticed Sarah standing on one of the balconies of the brothel after the long night hours of abuse. Her eyes transfixed on the crowds of people coming up the street, she appeared to be looking for something or someone. It was the only time Grant could recall seeing her face wearing the expression of hope.

"Sarah," Grant asked one day, "why do you stand on the balcony looking up the street in anticipation?"

"I'm waiting for my father to come and rescue me and take me home," she replied.

Little did she know that it was her father that sold her to the brothel; it was a small price for a nicer car. In the months that followed she contracted a deadly sexual disease and asked Grant to move her bed from her room to the flat brothel rooftop where she wanted to sleep at night.

While he was tucking her in one night, with the moonbeams setting her gaunt but still beautiful little face aglow, he asked her, "Sarah, why did you want to move up here to sleep? Was it so you can see the stars at night?"

"Not really," she whispered. "I want to be up here so my eyes can look up to heaven as I wait for my heavenly Father to come and rescue me, and take me home."

A couple of nights later little Sarah quietly slipped away into her eternal resting place. She doesn't have to imagine what heaven looks like anymore. Grant carried her lifeless body from the rooftop to prepare her for burial. I carry an image in my mind of what they both must have looked like as Grant stood with her fragile, delicate body in his arms under the Thai night sky. It makes me think of my favorite Michelangelo sculpture, the *Pieta*: Mary holding Jesus after his body was removed from the cross. I imagine a similar reverence as Grant held Sarah, one of "the least of these," an innocent one who *was wounded by our transgressions*, through our inactivity regarding issues of injustice, and *bruised by our iniquities* through our self-centered living and forgetfulness of the poor. But Sarah is now home, safe and held in the arms of love, while the flesh of our Lord is still torn through the wounds inflicted on mankind.

The image of Sarah, as well as the *Pieta*, make me wonder: How can God find in us the comforting warmth of a friend, and how can our love for others be a healing balm to His heart, a heart scarred and broken since the creation of man?

Your Story

Let's gain a better understanding of contemplative activism by looking at the life of a Christ-follower of the past, Theresa of Lisieux. Let's learn how to follow her example, as she followed Christ, while we discover our false self—the one who wants to rob us of this transformative journey.

Theresa of Lisieux was a French Carmelite nun who lived over a hundred years ago. Daily Theresa would meditate on a picture of the suffering Christ. She observed blood flowing across the side of His face and down His side. She sensed, through her contemplation, that the blood of Jesus was still flowing through suffering humanity and the many injustices inflicted on the innocent. She made a promise to spend her life serving those in need and exposing injustice. While gazing on the picture of Jesus her prayer was this, "I don't want His precious blood to be lost. I shall spend my life gathering it up for the good of souls. For to live from love is to dry His face."[17]

1. This week how can you blend contemplation with activism? In the chapters ahead we will be exploring different forms of both—putting legs to our prayers is the first step. Ask the Lord, who are "the least of these" in the geographical area in which you live? This week go to that person, or people, and be a messenger of hope and encouragement. By ministering to them you are comforting Him who is the creator of all life, and you are learning to *live from love*, as is the mandate of all Christ-followers.

"To pursue a vocation in any field without the perspective of the world's poor—where God's heart and good news is centered, is folly." Craig Greenfield, Director of Alongsiders International[18]

2. The beginning of this chapter introduces us to an illusionary person that is part of all of our lives called, "The False Self." We allow the subtle emergence of this artificial person in an effort to numb the pain of our past and as an attempt to prove to ourselves and others we are worth being loved and/or respected through what we do.

> "The false self is like a shadow attached to each of us. Its motivation is emotional happiness; its drivers are personal power and control, personal safety and security, personal esteem and affection."
>
> Dr. Micha Jazz [19]

Which of the above mentioned drivers is part of your false self?

Have a conversation with God about this, asking Him to shine the light of His Spirit of truth into your falsehoods and to expose your true authentic self. Let's begin to discover what Christian mystics refer to as "the face we already had before we were born, before we did anything right or wrong, before we started performing."[20] Let's come home to God's original design of us, His purest dream of our true selves.

Notes

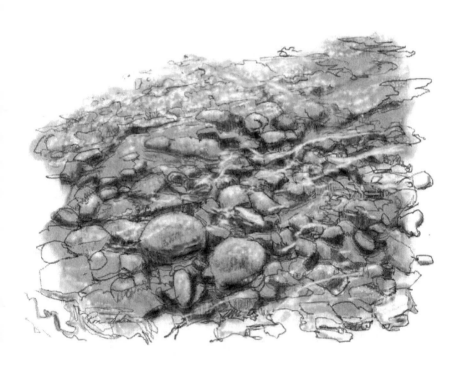

"There is no pit so deep, that God's love is not deeper still."

- Corrie Ten Boom, *The Hiding Place*

5

Being Looked at by Love

A whimsical look of reluctant joy flickered across Mom's face as she entered the living room. "After having six of you boys," she said to Gene and me, "I'm finally having a girl!" We were shocked. After bringing six boys into the world, we didn't think Mom and Dad were capable of producing a sister. "I've gotten very comfortable having boys." She continued, "What am I to do with a little girl?" We chuckled at the realization that she was both elated and apprehensive.

We were the "Pratt boys" until Nicole came along during our last few months in California. She became the crown jewel of the family. Nicole was Daddy's little princess, and her every desire was to win over his heart, though it had already happened the day she was born. The Pratt boys weren't quite as compliant, and we were well acquainted with the belt and the big spoon—the one that broke on the hindquarters of which child?

Our Northern California living experience ended more quickly than we had anticipated. Though we were smitten by its towering redwoods, blend of both sandy and rocky coastlines, and eclectic little towns framed by golden hills, its cultural values were contrary to our conservative, blue-collar family. California's accelerated pace of living, and what we perceived to be materialistic and egocentric mindsets, began to wear on our Pratt-family DNA. Even our Santa Rosa Mormon ward shared similar tendencies—experimental sex was common amongst its youth, a practice contrary to strong conservative Mormon values.

Our musical training from Brother Hicks was also coming to an end. "You all are a bit too squirrelly for this to work any longer," he said during his last session. "It's hard for you young ones to carry your harmonies without giggling, so come back when you have matured. Then I'll be happy to invest in you again."

We were in a state of transition. We packed our home yet again and moved to what would become the family favorite of our living destinations and the last of our frontiers as a family—the Pacific Northwest.

Baptizing the Dead

Typical of any Mormon young man wanting to be obedient to "the laws and ordinances of the Gospel," I became a priest at sixteen. I gave occasional sermons in front of the congregation and blessed the Sacrament of Communion. I was also expected to perform baptisms for the dead, which took place in one of the Mormon temples. I remember the honor of driving with other new priests to the Mormon Temple in Oakland, California to perform this ordinance.

I felt both strange and "holy," as I silently descended, all dressed in white, into the baptismal font. Waist deep in warm water, I stood in proxy for those who had died. I was baptized on their behalf, and this baptism gave each of them an opportunity to accept or reject the Mormon faith while they waited in the Spirit Prison. After being dunked in the water twenty times I felt waterlogged, exhilarated, and righteous for the wonderful good work I'd accomplished. I was a Mormon, and a good one at that.

Tremors of Change

Upon moving to Vancouver, Washington, we became immediately active, as was our norm, in our new Mormon ward. Occasionally, the Pratt Brothers sang in front of the congregation, and we busied ourselves with the typical activities that occupied the lives of devout teenage Mormons: seminary at 6:00 am, monthly church dances and sporting events, and weekend and mid-week meetings. However, Dad, Mom, and I missed the simple life alongside the shores of Mendocino Lake where we had experienced the presence of God. A thirst for a simpler, more meaningful spirituality had been awakened in our hearts. We could no longer exist with Jesus' story as only part of our lives; He had invited us to actually know Him—to live His story now. But we weren't even sure what that meant.

At the time we didn't think the church doctrines were wrong. Instead we thought we were not fulfilled spiritually in the Mormon Church because it was going through a state of apostasy, which meant it had strayed from its original beliefs—the centrality of Christ and an ever-growing relationship with Jesus as its cornerstone.

One Sunday evening, at a local Mormon Church leaders' meeting, my dad was asked to attend a Christian church service to hear a German friend, Mr. Ostermann, give a message. He was an inactive member of the Mormon Church, and the leaders wanted to see if he would be saying anything against Mormonism that would call for his ex-communication. But as it turned out, Mr. Ostermann didn't speak about the Mormon Church at all.

This was the first Christian church my parents attended since becoming Mormons. When they entered the service a few minutes late, probably because of Dad's *gift of gab*, they were immediately struck by how intimate the congregants were in their expression of worship to God. Some knelt down in reverence; others had their arms lifted up with tears rolling down their faces. My parents sensed the presence of God among the people. This experience led Mom to later attend a Christian Bible study and started my parents on a spiritual journey that would forever change my family's relationship with the Mormon Church and our understanding of God.

A year later Gene and I were invited to accompany Mom and Dad to a Christian church service. I was intrigued. What would it feel like to be in a Christian church (which I was taught) had only a portion of the truth? Most of my exposure to Christianity was through the writings of C.S. Lewis and the television evangelists my brothers and I watched for comic relief. Each take on the Christian life seemed very different from the other.

I will never forget that first Christian service I attended at Mountain View Christian Center in Ridgefield, Washington, an affiliate of the Assemblies of God. My reaction was the same as my parents a year earlier. I was struck by how intimately the people interacted with God during worship. It appeared as if they had a deep relationship and a real emotional connection with Him. I was raised with a profound reverence and respect for God but not much emotional interaction with Him. When we saw the congregants lifting their hands in the air, faces painted with expressions of true love and adoration, we were deeply moved. With complex Mormon doctrines as my only frame of reference for spirituality, this simple, beautiful devotion interested me. Eventually I began to attend Mountain View in the evening after teaching Sunday school at the Mormon Church in the morning—bringing my Book of Mormon to both.

Our family was first impressed by the vulnerability of Moutain View Christian Center. They didn't appear, or try to appear, to have everything together. The goal of our new Christian friends wasn't *perfection*, but rather learning how to love God more completely while acknowledging personal brokenness and the need for grace. This was a foreign concept to me. I despised neediness. Mormons rarely acknowledged needs because true believers had to reflect a religion that was flawless, one that had all the answers. But in those early years, a statement a Christian friend made to me confirmed what I found to be true: "Our need is the most precious possession we have outside of Jesus Christ Himself." Perfection wasn't a thing to be possessed; Christ was.

While interacting with my new Christian friends I found myself beginning to acknowledge my needs, my desire for intimacy and my longing for a Savior. During my first Christian testimony meeting, I remember standing up at Moutain View Christian Center and sharing a verse out of Alma, from The Book of Mormon that read, "I know that I am nothing, as to my strength I am weak, therefore I will not boast of myself but I will boast of my God, in whose strength I can do all things" (Alma 26:12a). Then everyone spoke a rousing "AMEN!" I'm sure they thought I was quoting just another verse out of the Bible.

Goodbye Mormon Life

In those days, I worked at *Kentucky Fried Chicken*, and one night, after a long shift, my car wouldn't start. My mom came to my rescue, and on the ride home, after we talked about what we were learning through our new Christian friends, mom pulled over to the side of the road, stopped the car, and became very serious.

"I know this is not going to be a big surprise to you Jeff," she said, "but your father and I have been praying and feel it's time for us to leave the Mormon Church." She paused, gathered her emotions, then continued. "We feel there's such a thirst in our hearts to know Jesus better, and as you know, we don't feel like we are being taught that in the Mormon Church. We are going to attend Mountain View Christian Center full time, but we don't want any of you kids to feel that you need to do the same. We are just asking you, Gene, Steve and Tim to pray and ask God where he would have you go. We will completely support whatever decision you make."

Mom already knew my decision. I felt an obligation to continue attending the Mormon Church Sunday services for a few months longer.

I was teaching a Sunday School class, and wanted to give the class an opportunity to begin a relationship with God. Within five months everyone in our family except for my brother Gene was attending the Christian church full-time.

Was it hard to say goodbye to my Mormon friends, to explain the direction we were taking? Yes. It seemed that most people left Mormonism because of moral failings, not because the church wasn't meeting their spiritual needs. And even when we left, I thought once we became rooted in our relationship with God we might return to Mormonism and lead others to know Him.

Portals of Grace

There are many ways to a spiritual awakening. For some, it's God's story written into the seasonal changes of creation that brings them into redemptive hope. For others it's a timely book or movie, a piece of artwork, a song capturing our attention, or the kind look of a friend. These are all portals of grace, which the Relentless Pursuer uses to draw us to Himself. In this season of my life it seemed that everything reflected to me the nature and character of a loving God.

Before I left the Mormon Church, and while driving home to Santa Rosa after performing baptisms for the dead at the Oakland temple, a friend named Mark said to me, "I heard a story the other day that makes me think about Jesus in the same way that you do. There was a single father who had two sons, Tom and Sam, who were eight and eleven years old. Their father was so selfish he would often forget to feed them, and he rarely spent time with them. Something happened to him that changed his life though; I guess he gave his life to God. People could tell he had changed because he began to take his sons with him everywhere, even to work. One weekend they went white water rafting. You've gone rafting before, right?"

"Yes," I replied, "It's one of my favorite outdoor activities."

"Well during their ride down the river," he continued, "after they finished going through a series of rapids, they pulled the boat to the shore for a nap. They didn't think there were any more rough waters until much later in the day. While they were asleep their raft hit a boulder, which caused the raft to capsize, dumping them into the rapids. One of his sons, Tom, was a good swimmer and made it to shore. The other son Sam was eight years old and didn't know how to swim. While Tom was on shore his eyes scanned the river for any sight of his dad or Sam. Then, to his shock, he suddenly saw his brother in the middle of the waves—he looked like he was standing on the water. While Mark stared in wonder, a helicopter came out of nowhere and lowered itself above Sam, lifting him into the cab. A minute later Tom fainted from shock and exhaustion.'"

Mark paused for a moment, as if he needed to process the stories' harrowing conclusion.

"The next morning Tom awoke in a hospital bed across from his brother. Relieved to be alive he said, 'Sam, how are you feeling? Where's Dad? Is he in the waiting room?'"

"Sam didn't respond for a moment and then painfully said, 'No. I was standing on Dad's shoulders.' I guess, Jeff, when the water of the river had receded, the body of their father was found at the bottom with one of his feet purposely wedged between two rocks."

"What a sacrifice this father made, what love," Mark said, obviously astonished. "That's like Jesus, like how you explained him to me. I want to know a love like that."

One evening, a few months later, I prayed a dangerous prayer: *God, show me my heart so I can understand Yours. I want to truly know what your Son did for me on the cross.* Late that night I had a dream that felt extremely real. In the dream the door to my room was pushed opened and thick waves of darkness proceeded to tumble in, like mighty torrents of a raging river. As the waves began to surround me, I recognized that they were carrying all the sin of my life—any evil I had surrendered to, in thought, word, or deed—I could suddenly remember. The awareness of the magnitude of my sins was too much for me to bear as those sins pressed against my neck. Eventually I could not fight them any longer, and I began to drown in my sin. At the moment I felt I was going to die, I heard my father say, "Whenever you need help, call out to God and He will always be attentive to your cry." I opened my mouth and whispered the words, "My Lord, my God, my Jesus, I'm sorry... forgive me for my sins and selfishness, my lust, my me. I need your help." Immediately, I felt something push me out of the darkness, and for the first time in my life I felt free. With ecstatic relief I looked down at my feet where the waves of my darkness, like a mighty river, were flowing against my ankles. I was so grateful I wasn't down there anymore. Then suddenly, to my shock, as I looked closer into the darkness beneath me, I realized I was standing on someone's shoulders. It was the figure of a man. I didn't recognize him, but he was visibly in extreme pain. Why? He was breathing in the sickness of my sins, taking into his lungs my darkness and impurities. My issues were suffocating and killing him as he rocked his head back and forth, gasping for air.

For a moment I thought, "Who are you, and why are you doing this for me? This isn't your sin." I felt like jumping off his shoulders, but I didn't want to re-enter my self-made hell. Then he lifted one of his hands out the darkness, and when my eyes rested on the nail prints, I realized who He was. My heart almost stopped beating— *Jesus, it's you*, I thought. He tilted his head up and looked at me. If there were any gaze all of humanity longs to come home to, it would be that look of love. The God of all compassion, power, and vulnerability was looking up at me—drowning in my sin. Though His mouth didn't move I heard Him speak to my heart and say, *I love you with an everlasting love and I long to call you my friend.* While transfixed by His gaze I made myself a promise: I'm going to spend the rest of my life knowing and loving You, Jesus, the one whose shoulders I stand on, and I'm going to communicate to others the price you paid for our Homecoming.

I woke early that morning, and the meaning of my dream was clear.

I was seldom honest with myself about my struggles; I preferred to believe all the good things people said about me. I craved respect. I could now see clearly the addicted state of my psyche, like a pendulum, swinging from self-doubt to pride and back again depending on the circumstances of my life. I became aware that I lived primarily for *me*. Even the good things in my life were attempts to get people to like me, to think I was spiritual or exciting and cool. For years I graded myself on a curve. Compared to most people I was looking pretty good. I was part of a Mormon family; many people wanted to emulate us. But that night all the illusions about myself became exposed, and I saw how desperately I needed to be rescued. I wanted a Savior more than I wanted to be a little god. However, far overshadowing these realizations was the earth-shattering reality that Love looked at me, *all of me*, and found me wanting and desirable, even in my ugliness.

Since God met me in the drama of my youth, speaking to me through dreams and imagery I could understand, I've come to believe a simple truth. No matter what hardships, suffering, or sin we encounter in this life, as Corrie Ten Boom said, "There is no pit too deep that God's love is not deeper still."[21]

I wish the vision I caught of Jesus that night, in His love and in His suffering would stay forever before my spiritual eyes. Is it possible to be transfixed by His gaze every day, where He becomes the lens through which we perceive all things? I've learned that the spiritual disciplines of Jesus make this kind of life possible. Will you continue exploring them with me?

Your Story

What led me to explore a Bible-based contemplative spirituality was the desire to live with a heart that was awakened to the love of Christ. I wanted the revelation of the Cross of Jesus and His sacrifice for me, which I experienced when I stood on His shoulders in my dream, to become an abiding, daily reality. I would like to lead you into a method of praying called contemplative prayer that can help make this possible, Let's learn how to be looked at by Love.

Contemplative prayer is a method of prayer that leads us into resting in God, a rest that is beyond thoughts, words and emotions. It's where we practice Psalm 46:10, "Be still and know that I am God." It is a movement beyond conversation with Christ to communion with Him. As Father Keating said, "Contemplative prayer is not a 'felt' presence of God (though you may feel Him at times), but is rather a deepening of faith in God's abiding presence." [22]

1. Let's begin. Sit comfortably and relax. Breath out the cares of your day. Now imagine God, the face of love, looking at you. Allow yourself to be looked at without having to respond with words—surrender to an intimacy that is beyond words where you take a vacation from yourself. Gaze upon the beauty of God with the eyes of your heart, as it says in Psalms 27:4, "in whom we live and move and have our being (Acts 17:28)." When distracting thoughts come, which they certainly will, meet them with stillness, not commentary—give the distracting thoughts a name (like worry, anger, lust, or distraction) and then let them go. [23]

2. Once you detach from distracting thoughts, you are no longer a victim of your thoughts, but a witness of them.[24] Then you simply, gently return to envisioning Christ, who is fully present and longs for our full presence. For some it's helpful to have a sacred word, a word that represents something personal between you and God. For example you might use Jesus, Abba, love, home or peace. After you detach from your thoughts, you simply whisper this word, and it will center you again into the arms of God.

3. Practice this method of prayer for five minutes a day for three days, then increase to ten minutes, gradually working your way to the typical twenty minutes that many believers around the world practice daily.

Notes

"The main business in this life is to restore to health the eyes of our hearts whereby God can be seen."

- St. Augustine of Hippo

6

The Eye of the Tiger

I have four days to experience a passionate bus romance, I thought as I entered the Greyhound bus station to investigate the route I would be taking from Vancouver, Washington, to Upstate New York. I didn't want to spend my high school graduation money to fly to visit my relatives, and I was certain the slow route would be a great adventure. *From the plethora of states we'd be passing through*, I thought, *the chances would be high I'd meet a tall blond willing to accompany me on my travels*. Filled with anticipation, and with an empty seat next to me, I left Vancouver and headed toward Idaho. Over the next few hours dozens of elderly people hobbled on and off the bus. *Where was she*, I thought? I lifted a desperate prayer, and to my amazement, eight excruciating hours into the bus ride, there she was.

She boarded the bus and all eyes turned to her tall, thin body. She was dressed like a ranch hand, and normally I wouldn't find that style attractive, but in this case it worked. She paused next to the driver for a moment to survey her seat options. I looked down, not wanting to appear too desperate, and reverently pleaded, "O God, if you sit her next to me, the days will go by so much faster!" A moment later I felt movement next to me. It was the ranch hand.

I wondered what to say, considered the old saying—aren't first impressions everything? If I didn't talk soon, things would get awkward. I wondered, *how could I be both funny and clever right off?*

As if on cue, a boy of about 12 years old who sat in front of us, gave me an excellent window of opportunity. Assuming we were together, he turned around and asked, "Where are you guys going?"

Without hesitation, I responded, "My wife and I are going to New York City."

There was just a moment's pause and then she said, "Yes, we're going there to pick up one of our children." *Children*, I thought, *I can do children, I love you already!* For the next hour and a half we talked to the boy, making up our lives along the way. Sometimes she even corrected me, "Excuse me, Hon," she said, "the second night of our honeymoon wasn't in Germany, but in Switzerland." Trying to hide my blushing I said, "That's right, who could forget that night!" We were getting far too intimate and didn't even know each other's names.

Nancy—I was soon to discover—was on her way to Buffalo, New York, to spend the summer working for a relative. She was a great conversationalist and had a lovely way of weaving intrigue and humor in her interesting banter about every state we passed through. She had obviously been on this bus route before.

Needless to say the trip went by more quickly than I had anticipated. When we got to Binghamton's bus station, I could see my grandparents getting off a bench to greet me. I began to gather my carry-on belongings. Saying goodbye to Nancy was sad. Over the course of just 48 hours, she'd won a piece of my heart.

Of course, these were the days when people actually wrote letters, and after three days of anxiously waiting to hear from her, I smelled perfume emanating from the mailbox. I ripped the top of the envelop off and read the first couple of sentences. They went something like this, "Jeff, my bus ride with you has radically changed my life." *Me too*, I thought, with a gasp! Then she continued, "Because of the passion of what you believe and how you shared your religion with me, I have left my Assembly of God church and have joined the Mormon Church."

I almost dropped the letter in ecstatic joy. I stopped there on my grandparent's driveway and thanked God for helping me lead a person (and a very pretty one at that!) into his true church.

What is a Christian?

I met Nancy almost a year before I started attending Moutain View Christian Center and pursuing Christianity as a way of life. But after making this decision, my letters to Nancy were returned. I couldn't find her. She moved, and there were no online tools to track her down in those days.

Before meeting Nancy, I already had a number of experiences with Jesus, but I still believed in the Mormon Church. And this story begs the question: What determines how much truth and error a person can believe to be considered a Christian?

I think Jesus has been pursuing us all of our lives—the moments we surrender to Him make an ongoing conversion possible. During my first year of attending Mount View Christian Center, spending time with God every day, I began to get to know His character and nature. The Mormon theology I believed began to fall away as I discovered that it was inconsistent with biblical truth. I stopped believing that I was going to be a god someday. Looking back, I am so thankful that my new Christian friends were patient with my process and didn't immediately tell me what to believe.

Sadly, that bus ride made it clear that my passion for Mormonism was greater than Nancy's devotion to Christianity. What did she see in me that made her want to leave her church? It wasn't Mormon theology; I hadn't mentioned any to her. In my whole-hearted devotion and counter-cultural way of living, she saw that I lived for something.

Passionate devotion, wherever it is found, is attractive and contagious in the world today. Everyone longs to give themselves absolutely and completely to a noble call and purpose. But today, I believe there is no greater noble call or purpose than knowing and following Jesus as *the* way of life.

Beautiful Beginnings & Subtle Compromises

I had a wondrous start as a church-attending believer. My friends in the youth group had an active spirituality and focused not only on loving God but also loving one another well. They helped me learn to become less awkward and lavished their affection on me whether or not I knew how to receive it.

I drank in every church service and conference, from Bill Gothard seminars to Pentecostal Holy Spirit meetings, where I responded to altar calls and was slain in the Spirit (which is to say I was pushed down by the preacher). Those initial Christian events and church experiences were adventurous and invigorating. I loved the various expressions of Christianity.

After attending Christian services for a year and a half, I started speaking in youth groups. I liked the attention and identity I received from being a converted Mormon priest. And though I wanted the best of what I felt God had to offer, I also held the same desire for things of the world. There were competing loyalties in my heart. When I walked into a clothing store I was immediately attracted to the highest priced items. At Christmas or on birthdays, I returned gifts and purchased more expensive things. I owned two leather jackets (which is still a family joke today). I was raised in a blue-collar family, but I didn't want to look like it.

At the time I had accepted minor leadership roles at Mountain View Christian Center. As one of the coordinators for the children's church, the nature of my work drew me closer to examining the institution of church and the faithfulness of its people. Church members who had lifted their hands in great abandon one week were exposed for infidelities the next—deeply respected church leaders were no exception. This was a major shock to my family and me because everyone appeared to be so close to God in their demonstrative styles of worship and charismatic testimonies. Yet several of those who had made grave mistakes later admitted that one of their compromises was being too busy for regular communion times with God. Why didn't the people of God make time for Him; how could they become so complacent?

Dad and Rocky III

In my late teens and early twenties my dad and I rarely connected emotionally. I loved him dearly, but I wondered if he really *got* me. One night I asked him if he'd like to see the movie *Rocky 3* with me. As an aspiring journalist, I was taking a film appreciation course at Clark College and was beginning to specialize in writing movie reviews. And though I didn't think another Rocky movie would be a profound film experience (I was in the mood for a fun, mindless flick), I had no idea what a catalytic effect this movie would have on my life.

In the film, having defeated Apollo Creed and spoiled with the excesses of being the heavyweight champion of the world, Rocky lost his fighting edge. Everyone loved him, and yet he was the coddled celebrity with fixed fights so he could hold on to the title. Then entered James "Clubber" Lang, a powerhouse fighter whom everyone loved to hate. Clubber Lang didn't care what anyone thought; his passion to be the champion was all consuming. Rocky was protected from fighting Clubber because the Italian Stallion's coach didn't think he was strong enough to beat the hungry bruiser. But in his pride, Rocky agreed to the fight and ultimately lost.

In the wake of the loss, Rocky's coach and wife challenged him to get his game back, to recover the passion he had lost. They encouraged him to leave the glitz and glamour of the environment where he had been training and return to his old gym, outside the spotlights, where he could give all of himself once again to recapture the steely determination he once had—*the eye of the tiger.*

Dad and I watched, riveted as Rocky came roaring back to regain the title. The concluding music and credits hypnotically glued us to our seats. Afterwards we went to a pie shop, and while eating slices of Raspberry sour cream pie, Dad said, "Son I know you love God, and your mother and I are proud of you." He paused and I could tell from his tone, *things can only go down from here.* "However you also care deeply about other things." He continued, as he rolled a bit of his piecrust around his plate. "Image and nice things are important to you," he said. "With your drive and tenacity I know you will attain whatever you put your mind to in life." Then with a melancholy look he said, "I remember when you used to run. You had a look in your eyes, a passion and determination that made you win almost every time. Can you imagine what it would be like if you had that same passion for God, if you loved Him with all your heart, mind, and strength—if you had an eye single to His glory, the eye of the tiger?"

I stared at the condensation on my cup of ice water, listening. I knew every word was true. I was not offended or discouraged by his words. In fact, a fire began to burn in my bones, a wild hope I had never experienced. *Imagine if I could love God like that,* I thought, *if I could love Him with everything, and live with a passion for His satisfaction and glory instead of my own.*

A few days later the family was getting ready to take a summer road trip back to New York. Some of the kids hadn't seen their relatives in some time, so the plan was to visit both sides of the family for a month. While everyone loaded up the van Dad asked, "Where is your luggage?" I wasn't sure how to answer, so I quickly said, "I'm not going."

Shocked he asked, "Don't you want to see everyone?"

"O yes, it'd be great fun," I said," but I need to stay."

He put down the luggage he was holding and leaned against the van to listen to me. "I'm giving God one month of my life," I said, "a month where I will seek Him with all of my heart, mind and strength. If I find Him to be all that He says He is, I will serve Him all the days of my life. If not, I'll still be a Christian, but I'll also pursue other things—become great at something."

There was a long silence. Then came that look on Dad's face, the look I saw every time I had passed the finish line and won a race. "Ok, Son," he said. "We'll miss you and so will your relatives, but there is nothing more important you can do with your time."

Dad told me years later that when they all waved goodbye to me, and the green van pulled out of the St. Johns driveway to head for the East Coast, they were waving to a person they would never see again; the me they used to know would soon pass away.

Repentance - Encounter - Awakening

What does a month with God look like? I wasn't sure. The morning after we saw *Rocky 3*, I opened my Bible and my eyes fell upon Revelation 2:4-5, "Yet I hold this against you: You have forsaken the love you had at first. Remember the height from which you have fallen! Repent and do the things you did at first." A burning conviction flooded my heart, and I knew I needed to return to the spiritual gym and reclaim the furious fervency and passion I had when I first found God. This unction didn't come with an agonizing striving component—my month was not about *trying* to find God, but about *training*. I would pray in the words of St. Augustine, "restore to health the eyes of my heart whereby God can be seen." [25]

I knew various layers of myself were obscuring my view of God. Somehow these layers needed to be acknowledged, to be put to rest and to die. I read Oswald Chambers' depiction of a white funeral—*the burial of the old life*—in *My Utmost for His Highest*, and it captured the need in my life for spiritual renewal. In it, Chambers writes, "Have you come to your last days really? There must be a 'white funeral,' a death that has only one resurrection—a resurrection into the life of

Jesus Christ. Nothing can upset such a life, it is one with God for one purpose, to be a witness to Him." [26]

During my first mornings of prayer before I went to work, I began contemplating the personal death that I needed. My *training* began by slowly reading the opening passage of Romans 6, which reads, "What shall we say, then? Shall we go on sinning so that grace may increase? By no means! We died to sin; how can we live in it any longer? Or don't you know that all of us who were baptized into Christ Jesus were baptized into his death?"

I meditated on the verses of Roman 6, and it became my "white funeral." I envisioned my own casket. With every realization of what Jesus accomplished for me, I walked to the casket and laid down the parts of my false self I allowed to remain alive.

I was painfully specific. Hair has always been a big deal to me. I'd wash it, spray it and gel it, until it was exactly the look I wanted. So into my casket went my comb, representing my over self-consciousness with body image. Accompanying my comb was my black leather jacket, which represented my attachments to the nice things that made me feel more valuable. I emptied all my falseness and found I had more mental and emotional space for God to fill.

This process of purification wasn't about striving to get God to forgive me or change me, though; I already had years of experience with the goal of godhood and perfection. My heart's cry was a desire to know and find God above all else—whatever the cost. This led me to study how an encounter with God takes place in the Bible. During my scripture readings I saw that John the Baptist's mission was to prepare the way of the Lord through a call to repentance. I also noticed that when Isaiah encountered God in his holiness, Isaiah immediately recognized that he was a man of unclean lips. After he repented and was forgiven he overheard a missional call proposed as a question, "Who will go for me?" [27]

In the pages of Scripture, I saw a recurring biblical theme: repentance—a change of direction in where we are looking for happiness—precedes a spiritual awakening. Spiritual awakening leads to the discovery of Christian activism. I wanted to follow in the steps of those who'd gone before me, so repentance and prayer became my pathway home to an awareness of my union with God and His dreams for my life. It became my doorway to Christian activism.

There are moments in life when we realize something beautiful has been done for us. This is true of spiritual awakening. In spiritual awakening, we realize we already have everything we need. After my "white funeral" purification experience, I began to read the books of Ephesians and Colossians. Occasionally I would pray the scriptures; other times I would read, wait, and listen. Throughout the month my spiritual eyes opened afresh to my place in God's redemptive story—a life of less trying and more trusting, less struggling and more resting in the One in whom "we live and move and have our being." [68]

Our focus determines our experience, every time. This "Eye of the Tiger" season in which I wholeheartedly sought God steered my focus back to taking responsibility for my story so I could begin to live His. This event didn't change me forever and wasn't a quick fix; it was part of the struggle and beauty of an ongoing conversion.

It's this ongoing conversion that keeps me coming back to God for the often-painful process of restoring to health the eyes of my heart. To this day it inspires me towards a passionate devotion that eclipses the love I had for Mormonism.

The Miracle of the Not So Empty Chair

Years later I was challenged by a story of the wholehearted devotion of an elderly man dying of cancer. [28] The old man's daughter asked the local priest to come and pray with her father. When the priest arrived, he found the man lying in bed with his head propped up on two pillows and an empty chair beside his bed. The priest assumed that the old fellow had been informed of his visit. "I guess you were expecting me," he said.

"No, who are you?"

"I'm the new associate at your parish," the priest replied. "When I saw the empty chair I figured you knew I was coming."

"Oh yeah, the chair," said the bedridden man. "Would you mind closing the door?"

Puzzled the priest shut the door.

"I've never told anyone this, not even my daughter," said the man, "but all my life I have never known how to pray. It always went right over my head. Until one day, four years ago, my best friend said to me, 'Joe, prayer is just a simple matter of having a conversation with Jesus. Here's what I suggest. Sit down on a chair; place an empty chair in front of you, and in faith see Jesus on the chair. It's not spooky because he promised, 'I'll be with you always.' Then just speak to him and listen in the same way you're doing with me right now.' So Padre, I tried it and I've liked it so much that I do it a couple of hours every day. But I'm careful because if my daughter saw me she would send me off to the funny farm."

The priest was deeply moved by the story and encouraged the old man to continue on the journey. Then he prayed with him, anointed him with oil, and returned to the rectory.

Two nights later the daughter called to tell the priest that her father had died that afternoon.

"Did he seem to die in peace?" he asked.

"Yes, when I left the house around two o'clock, he called me over to his bedside, told me one of his corny jokes, and kissed me on the cheek. When I got back from the store an hour later, I found him dead. But there was something strange, Father. In fact beyond strange, kind of weird. Apparently just before Daddy died, he leaned over and rested his head on a chair beside his bed."

After sharing this story at a retreat I was leading in Dunham, Quebec, I sent everyone away to seek God in silence and solitude for a few hours of prayer. There was a French couple in the midst of marital struggles. They came to the retreat hoping they would have a life-altering encounter with God.

After an hour of prayer the husband came out of the forest with tears in his eyes. He said, "Come, I have to show you something." We hiked deep into the woods and found a tranquil babbling brook. He explained to me, "In desperation I knelt down in front of this stream right here to pray, saying to God 'I can't imagine that you would want to be with me after all of the bad things I've done in my life.' Then I lifted my eyes up, feeling the powerful presence of someone close by, and look what I saw." There in the middle of the stream facing us was an empty chair.

The Open Wound of Love

"The heart of God is an open wound of love," says Richard Foster, "He aches over our distance and preoccupation. He weeps over our obsession with muchness and manyness. He longs for our presence." [29] In the days of my own white funeral, in the many white funerals I've witnessed over the years, the truth of Foster's statement is clear.

Here, let's slow down and contemplate God's open wound of love and examine our own personal stories. Let's make space for the death of our own false selves, for repentance, and a re-birth of radicalism in our pursuit of God. Let's acquire eyes set on His glory, that we may be able to say with Paul, in Galatians 2:20, "I have been crucified with Christ and I no longer live, but Christ lives in me. The life I live in the body, I live by faith in the Son of God, who loved me and gave Himself for me." Let's make empty chairs for Him, let's live as if He's sitting there.

Your Story

Remember the first time you encountered the Lord and the season in life when He was your first love? Remember your spiritual thirst for God and how nothing else seemed to matter but your relationship with Him and loving those around you. Are you there now? As Oswald Chambers said, "Have you come to your last days really?" When we struggle with old ways of thinking and living, it's time for a spiritual renewal. Set aside a period of time, maybe a weekend or a month, and follow the guide below, implementing any of the spiritual disciplines, as you feel led to do so.* Believe in the capability of our God to *make all things new.*

1. Begin your first prayer time by initiating the purification process that precedes encounter. Begin your *white funeral* with the prayer of David found in Psalm 139:1, "O Lord you search me and you know me." Then slowly read Psalms 51 and 32, personalizing the text and inserting your own prayers along the way. Imagine, and draw a little coffin, that you symbolically put parts of yourself in that you are surrendering to God— as you take responsibility for the parts of your story that have been marred by selfishness and sin. Without guilt or shame, receive His forgiveness.

2. Prepare for encounter. Surround yourself with the beauty of creation and read the books of Ephesians and Colossians. Meditate on any verses that stand out to you. As part of your spiritual training, memorize several of those verses so you can bring them to mind throughout your work day.

3. Begin and end each day of your renewal with a time of worship, allowing your waking and retiring moments to be with the Lord and not online. Consider inviting a friend to join you for this season of spiritual renewal.

Something Old Something New
Yearning for a new way will not produce it.
Only ending the old way can do that.
You cannot hold onto the old, all the while
declaring that you want something new.
The old will defy the new;
The old will deny the new;
The old will decry the new.
There is only one way to bring in the new.
You must make room for it.
Neal Donald Walsch [30]

*The classical spiritual disciplines can be listed in two categories, the inner and outer, as listed in Richard Foster's classic book, *The Celebration of the Disciplines.*[31]

The inner spiritual disciplines are prayer, silence and solitude, biblical meditation, Scripture study, fasting, worship and celebrating. The outer spiritual disciplines are confession, giving and service.

Notes

"How can you be so dead, when you've been so well fed? Jesus rose from the grave, and you can't even get out of bed!"

- Keith Green, "Asleep in the Light"

7
Missional Dreams

Little Johnny had a fixation with Tarzan. He would often arrive at His Lit'l Bodies Shoppe Preschool, where I worked in college, and he'd run straight to the bathroom. After closing the door and locking it, he'd take off his clothes and wrap a towel around his waist—his imaginary leopard-skin loincloth. He'd throw the door open and run into his make-believe jungle, swinging from the curtains as if they were vines. Normally this ritual was no big deal to us. We recognized it as just another of Johnny's hyperactive routines. We were especially patient with him, knowing that he was a battered child adopted into a Christian home. But today was picture day, and it was work enough to gather everyone else to get a good school picture without chasing Johnny.

All the kids showed up that morning dressed to the nines. Some of the girls had curled hair, and even Johnny was wearing a white shirt with a little black vest. So when he got to the bathroom for his routine of transforming into Tarzan and found the door locked, he was very disturbed. Quickly I said, "Johnny, I really need your help." He looked at me with an exaggerated pout and a suspicious look. "Please help me round up the kids so we can get a good group picture; then maybe we can invite Tarzan to join us for snack time later on!" Johnny instantly became helpful (and bossy). But I achieved my desired results, and all the kids were in rows in front of the pine trees in the backyard. *The parents are going to love this picture*, I thought. Even Johnny was standing front and center and very calm, with a wry wicked grin on his face. I should've gotten suspicious; he was never that still.

Just before the Body Shoppe manager snapped the photograph, Johnny dropped his pants to his knees and began to pee on everyone standing around him. He must have had a gallon of lemonade that morning, and I must give it to him—he was a good shot. Immediately everything went from order to a riotous circus. The girls started to scream and tripped over one another as they ran to the bathroom. When I tried to help them wash the pee out of their hair, Justine burst into tears and said, "Teacher Jeff, it got into my mouth!" I angrily looked over at Johnny who was curled up on one of the beanbags with both a smug and fake repentant look on his face.

This job sucks! I thought. What am I doing here?

Johnny's grand wiz experience happened a couple of months before I saw *Rocky* with my father. It affected not only how I saw God and myself, but also my perception of those around me. Before the renovation of my heart took place, my patience with the children at the preschool had grown progressively thinner. I usually couldn't wait to see my work hours come to an end so I could go to class. Now I found it hard to concentrate on my schoolwork and journalism studies. What had captivated me before had suddenly diminished. I began to look forward to the mornings teaching and playing with the kids, even being with crazy little Johnny. Though I no longer found the content of my college classes interesting, it was my fellow students, and what I perceived to be the state of their hearts, that now gave me a great sense of mission.

That's when the epiphany hit. *If I could spend all my time just loving people and sharing the wild wonders of my God with those around me, I would be the happiest person alive!*

During this period of my life, there was one person whose music and messages embodied what I felt the life of a Jesus-follower should look like: revivalist-musician Keith Green. I was spellbound every time I heard him speak and watched him sing as he pounded on his keyboard much like a warrior would his drum—his whole being consumed with the fury of his war cry against a life of nominalism and compromise. Keith made the spiritual revolution that he was demanding of the church seem irresistible.

"Do you see, do you see
all the people sinking down,
Don't you care, don't you care,
are you gonna let them drown?
How can you be so numb,
not to care if they come,
You close your eyes
and pretend the job's done.

But He cries, He weeps, He bleeds,
and He cares for your needs
And you just lay back and keep soaking it in,
Oh can't you see it's such sin!
The world is sleeping in the dark
that the church can't fight
cause it's asleep in the light.
How can you be so dead
when you've been so well fed?
Jesus rose from the grave
but you can't even get out of bed!" [32]

Keith was tragically killed in a plane accident with two of his children and a group of close friends. His last recorded concert was a challenge for the church to wake up and respond to the Great Commission, to make disciples of all nations. My response to Keith's fiery challenge and contagious passion made me one of over 100,000 people who committed their lives to full-time mission service during his memorial concerts in the fall of 1982.

I went to the Memorial Concert in Portland, Oregon, and at the end of the show, ushers passed out brochures for Youth With A Mission's flagship called the Anastasis, which was the Greek word for *resurrection*. I had an instant realization when I looked at the brochure and when I heard Keith's widow Melody Green speak about their organization *Last Day Ministries*. I knew both ministries would become part of my life's story.

After thorough research of Youth With A Mission (YWAM) I found its vision—*To know God and to make Him known*—resonated with my desire to be trained for full-time Christian service. No other vocation appealed to me. With my recent spiritual awakening and my deepening love for people, it only seemed natural for me to consider attending YWAM's entry-level five-month program, which was known as a Discipleship Training School (DTS). The first three months of DTS concentrated on personal transformation and how to develop a deep, intimate relationship with God. The last two months were a mission outreach where I'd put into practice what I'd learned.

There is nothing I'd rather do with my life, I remember thinking, as I finished reading the information about the DTS at His Little Body Shop. Then I paused and thanked God for my Mormon upbringing that made it easy for me to consider living for eternity, which instilled the principles of mission into my heart.

Dreams of God

Have you ever experienced *déjà vu*, a time or a place where everything seemed magically familiar, even home-like? Could it be that you were living out a dream God had for you, "good works that God prepared beforehand that we should walk in them" (Eph. 2:10)? I have found life is a beautiful mix between finding and walking out God's dreams for us, and when our lives become *movies in the making*, and we create our own dreams in partnership with Him.

Just before beginning the DTS, my friend Jerry was a part of a miraculous, inspirational story. Jerry was walking in front of a medical clinic on the outskirts of Las Vegas when he doubled over in pain on the sidewalk. Jerry was a competitive surfer in excellent physical condition, but these stomach cramps brought him to his knees. Two nurses from the clinic noticed him writhing in pain, brought out a stretcher, lifted Jerry onto it and carried him into the clinic for an immediate examination. While they called his parents and checked on his insurance, they set him next to a woman who was waiting for her appointment. Jerry began to pray, *God, is there a purpose behind this pain? Is there something you want to show me?* He heard the heart-whisper of God say, "Jerry you are feeling in your stomach my longing and pain for the lady that is sitting next to you. Open up your mouth and share my heart with her."

First he felt uncertain and wondered if it was God speaking. He also knew that the Bible said "no one is good but God alone," so he concluded that the selfless thoughts must be from God. Jerry said to the woman, "Excuse me Miss, God wants you to know that He dreams of you, and part of His dream is that you know He is madly, deeply in love with you—but not only with you, but also with the little one you carry in your womb. If that little one were to die, the heart of God would be broken."

Jerry didn't know that this woman was just getting ready to be taken into the next available room to have her baby aborted. Yet when she heard about a God who wasn't a distant judge sitting on a throne on a far side of the universe, but a God who was dreaming about her and the little one she was carrying in her womb, she walked out of that clinic with my friend Jerry.

Today that woman's son is a faithful follower of Jesus. He owes his life to a man who lived in a perpetual state of listening and responding—a contemplative activist. The Father is able to say of Jerry, "I no longer call you a servant, for a servant doesn't know what his master is doing. I call you my friend, because everything I hear from my Father I make known to you" (John 15:15).

Upon hearing this story I thought, *The DTS will train me how to be a friend of Jesus, not just His servant. Can there be any greater honor in this life?* Then I wondered, *How will my parents react if I don't finish college right now and launch out into such an unpredictable, radical life of faith?*

An End of An Era

That year, while I attended Clark College, there were tremors of change happening in our family. Gene was prepared to leave on his Mormon mission to Spain for two years, and Steve joined the Navy. A Pratt family era was coming to an end; no longer would we seven kids live in the same house or town ever again. With our numerous moves over the years and love for travel and camping, our thirst for adventure was now leading us older brothers out to see the world, leaving Tim home with the Dream Team.

Dad was the first person I told about my desire to attend the DTS, with a plan to finish my degree afterwards. "Son," he said with the warmth of a father's assurance, "As I consider all that God has done in your life the past six months, your plan sounds right and good. Now you need to explain this to your mother. You know how she feels about completing things that you start."

He gave me his approval (but not consent) and left the verdict to Mom. I was nervous. My mother was ever the pragmatist. Though I knew Mom's look of empowerment and love, I was well acquainted with her judgmental and disappointed gaze as well, the look I avoided at all costs. However, when I sat down and shared the passion I had to learn God's character and to experience a five-month adventure of being a missionary, the ole risk-taker Mom that we all knew and loved rose up within her. "I'm jealous," she said, "I want to go!" Before she could say another word and to appease her concerns about my future, I quickly interjected, "After the five-month journey I'll return and finish my journalism degree."

"Where will your YWAM training be?" she asked.

"Salem, Oregon, is the closest base. But I hope I save enough money to go to a cross-cultural DTS in Maui, Hawaii."

Mom smiled, "Hawaii! That's the one to do, isn't it?"

Then she asked cautiously, "What happens if you go that far and find out that YWAM is a cult?"

I paused and rolled my eyes for a moment before confidently saying, "Well, then at least I'll come back with a good tan and know how to surf! Besides Mom, the cheapest way to live in Hawaii is to take a DTS, so cult or not it's a no brainer!"

A week later my parents, several friends and I were invited to hear a prophetic Messianic Jewish preacher speak in a nearby church. His message was both meaningful and challenging. However, typical to my personality, I became critical and skeptical when he began to prophetically speak over the lives of certain individuals. I thought, *This Christian fortune-teller must memorize this stuff. If a person looks like they match the word he pulled out of his spiritual hat than he'd amaze them with his supposed discernment.* So I said a silent prayer, *God I know you have called me to missions for this period of my life. If this is a man of God please confirm that call through him.*

When I opened my eyes, the preacher was pointing at me. He said, "Young man, God has placed His hand on your life; He has called you to go. Drop what you have been doing and respond to the call. Go into all the world and preach the gospel!"

I couldn't move; I was awestruck. An army of goose bumps scurried up my arms and shoulders. He continued, "Much has happened in your life the past six months. Now is the time for you to step into the power of God's dreams for your life."

Over the next six months, through financial gifts and funds I had saved from work, I had enough money to attend a fall YWAM DTS, in Salem, Oregon. I would have needed an additional nine hundred dollars to attend the school in Maui, Hawaii. Having exhausted all my resources, I trusted that either location would accomplish the same goal of teaching me how to be a friend of God. *I'll have to learn how to surf later,* I thought. But while attending a Wednesday night service at Moutain View Christian Center, a close friend of the family approached me and said that God had prompted her to give me a financial gift for my DTS. She handed me a check and I stuck it in my pocket. *It's probably fifty dollars,* I thought, *enough for me to apply for my passport.* However, when I opened it later that day as I walked up the driveway to my house, my eyes widened and I almost lost my footing.

"Hey Mom," I yelled, as she pulled up behind me in the van. "Aloha... Hawaii here I come!"

The check was for nine hundred dollars.

Mangoes, Macadamia Nuts, and Me

How can a discipleship training school in Maui, Hawaii be bad? Though I didn't find YWAM to be a cult, one of my fellow students thought I was a Mormon spy sent to infiltrate the mission. What pearls of wisdom would I supposedly glean from YWAM that could help the Mormons in their mission of global domination? Surely not their organizational abilities—YWAM was less than efficient and as an organization could learn much from the Mormon writer Stephen Covey's book, *7 Highly Effective Habits for Highly Effective People.*

Aside from this minor hiccup, however, the wholehearted emphasis on deepening my relationship with God and learning to translate His love to the world was nothing short of revolutionary. I joined the DTS with a very privatized Christianity—it was God and I against the world. I had a disciplined relationship with him and didn't feel a need to include others in my intimate, slightly narcissistic spirituality. I was a professional at using God to solve my problems instead of using my problems to find God. At the beginning of the DTS, I hoped God would fix me; I learned that He's more interested in finding me in my brokenness and in finding others in their brokenness.

Due to my natural bent towards independence, the *we* verses of the Bible had always pushed me out of my comfort zone. "Since we are surrounded by such a great cloud of witnesses," the Scriptures say, "let us throw off all the sins that so easily entangle us… " (Heb. 12:1). Personally I'd rather do that on my own. Here's another—"As we walk in the light as he is in the light we have fellowship with one another," resulting in the promise that, "the blood of Jesus will cleanse us from all unrighteousness" (1 John 1:7).

These *we* verses insinuate that there is no real friendship or cleansing without the risk of being known. I had spent years being known by God, as is the challenge of 1 Corinthians 8:3, "…whoever loves God is known by God." But I didn't place a priority on *being known to others*. That was about to change.

During a time of prayer at the beginning of the DTS, I felt the sense that I would not experience the felt presence of God until I entered into open and honest relationship with others and found that He lives there too. I didn't realize I still wore independence as a protective cloak, as I had as a Mormon. This tendency slowly lost its grip as I encountered true humility in the life of others, as I met new friends and school leaders. I saw others risk being known for who they really were. Such true humility was rarely modeled in primary leadership positions in Mormon or Christian Churches.

The practice of intercessory prayer also pushed me towards a spirituality that was more others-focused. We learned to walk through a series of steps, to mentally silence the voice of self and the enemy, and listen to the voice of God. We'd ask Him to reveal His concerns and His heart for the world and those around us. After the listening phase we shared any impressions we had with our prayer team and assessed its connection to what anyone else may have heard or sensed. Then we prayed. Rarely did I sense anything from God in this context, but as the lecture phase of the school progressed, I received a recurring image of a tropical village perched on a hilltop. I began to wonder if the mental picture was divinely initiated because of its gentle consistency. I began to pray weekly for whoever lived in that village, that they would experience the life transforming power of the gospel.

But our DTS wasn't only about the inner and outer practices of prayer. We engaged in the mission of Jesus. In fact, it was our mission outreach to the Fiji Islands in the South Pacific that ruined me for the ordinary.

On the day my story began to merge with the Fijian people, Kim (one of my outreach leaders) and I were evangelizing on the outskirts of Fiji's largest city, Suva, on the island of Viti Levu. We turned the bend of a dirt road and on top of a hill before us was a cluster of shanty shacks with palm trees dispersed amongst the make-shift homes. The familiar configuration and size of the village astonished me. *That's it*, I thought—*the village I've seen during intercession—the village and people I have been praying for.*

"Let's take the gospel to that village, "I said to Kim. She gave an approving smile, and with great interest we began to follow the well-worn dirt trail up the hillside. Halfway up several Fijian youths accompanied us, chatted with Kim and me in relatively clear English as they helped us up parts of the rocky path. Their welcoming, disarming smiles and gentle demeanor made us feel immediately at home. When we reached the top of the hill, a warm fragrant breeze that smelled of curry spices and pineapples stirred up the palms around us and sent their branches waving.

"Wow," I said as I turned around and saw the sprawling city of

Suva beneath us. Most of the buildings were hidden under rich tropical greenery and framed on the horizon by the crashing turquoise waves of the South Pacific. "This is the life," I exclaimed, "suffering for the Lord in Fiji!"

We were led immediately into one of the huts, one composed of scrap pieces of wood, metal and tin. A friendly audience of eight people of various ages greeted us. They wore floral or bamboo shoot sulus wrapped around their waists and little else. One of them cooked fish on a small burner. His eyes met mine, and he handed me a half-opened coconut. After several jovial introductions and chit chat about where we were from, they inquired, "Why are you here? Why have you come up to our village?"

"We're Christian missionaries," Kim replied, "here to tell you about the love of God." Their eyes lit up in interest and one of the older listeners said, "We have to take you to meet someone." They all instantly nodded in agreement and led us out of their hut to a larger dwelling in the center of the village. We knocked on the door and all our new friends immediately vanished! We were to soon discover that this was the chief's hut. What was to transpire next would alter the destiny of both the village and my life.

Your Story

It says in Ephesians 2:10, "We are God's handiwork, created in Christ Jesus for good works, which God prepared in advance for us to do." Have you been awakened to God's missional dreams for your life, dreams that you were born to live out? I will guide you through a practice that will help you position your heart so that you can become aware of these dreams, and any potential dream stealers.

Contemplative Intercessory Prayer is seeking the presence and audience of God on behalf of a people or place, as we position our hearts to dream with the Divine Dreamweaver (1 Tim. 2:1-6). Follow these steps of intercession:

1. After a time of worship ask the Spirit to search you and know you, and see if there are fears or obstacles in your life that may hold you back from believing that God can use you to fulfill his dreams in the world— no matter how small or big those dreams may be. Clutch your fists in front of you and imagine that the besetting issues God reveals to you are things you are holding in your hands. While confessing these things to Him open your hands as a sign that you are letting them go. Then receive from God forgiveness, greater faith and whatever you need to proceed in hope.

2. Ask God to remind you of the good works of your past, His dreams you've already accomplished. Thank Him for how he used you and for the lives you were able to touch. Take a moment and intercede on their behalf.

3. With a heart of gratitude and surrender wait on God and ask Him to reveal to you His dreams and who and what is on His heart today. Allow your mind to roam through your neighborhood, a nearby city and out into the world. Don't be discouraged if you don't receive any impressions from Him at first, but make it your aim this week to carve out space to continue to intercede. You may want to add the spiritual discipline of fasting as you pray knowing, as it says in Hebrews 11:6, that "He rewards those who diligently seek Him."

Notes

" Blessed are the pure in heart
for they shall see God."

- Jesus, Matthew 5:8

8
The Eternal Gift of Fiji

Kim and I stood at the door of the chief's hut with fearful expectancy. Why had our newfound Fijian friends abandoned us so quickly after leading us here? After knocking just once the door quickly opened about five inches, to reveal half of a shriveled up face of what looked like a 125-year-old islander.

"What do you want," he grunted?

We paused for a moment, startled at being addressed so abruptly after such a warm welcome to the village.

"Are you Jehovah's Witnesses or Mormons?"

Used to be, I thought.

"Leave your Bibles, Book of Mormons, and papers and go back down the hill."

Unsure how to respond, we stared blankly at him for a moment. Then Kim quickly handed him one of our Christian tracts as I stood there curiously looking into his hut.

"You don't want to come in here," the chief said, looking at me in particular. He stepped back and threw the door open, revealing most of his living accommodations. "This isn't a nice place like where you are from," he said.

There was no furniture in view, just a couple of large wicker mats on the floor and a few pots and pans in the corner of the room with flies buzzing around them. Faded photos of what looked like family and friends hung in groupings on various parts of the wall.

"Yes we do want to come in," I said, taking a step into his home. The chief paused for a moment in surprise, then his features softened as he welcomed us.

"Then come, come in," he said.

The chief introduced us to his wife and then explained that he needed to interpret our conversation in order for her to properly understand. In typical Fijian style we sat on the living room wicker mat with our legs appropriately crossed, Kim and I facing them.

"Welcome to our home. It is nice to meet you," he said with little expression and in broken but clear English. We sat, looking at one another for a moment. I was overjoyed to be in the presence of the chief, to sit in a scene of what I'd always imagined the mission field to be. I didn't know what to say or where to begin, so I stammered, "Tell us about yourselves, your family and your beautiful village."

The chief beamed and in an animated fashion he began to tell us the story of his family and village. Every once in a while his wife would interject a detail that he would interpret for us. I was fascinated by the whole experience and felt like I could listen to them for hours.

After serving us tea, the chief sat back down and in a serious tone said, "Many years people have come to the top of our hill. They give us books and papers, but no foreigner has ever come in to sit on our floor and to be our friends. Why have you come? Is there any hope from your world to ours?"

Kim and I glanced at each other, overwhelmed at the natural ease of this invitation to speak of the Hope of all hopes. "We're here to talk with you about Jesus," I said, "about what it means to have a relationship with Him."

We joyfully shared the Gospel message with the chief and his wife, and they hung on our every word. After an hour of conversation the chief said, "Many years ago we had other missionaries come to our islands. We've always thought we are good Christians. But as we've listened to you we've come to understand that we have Jesus living up here," he said while he pointed to his forehead, "but not down here." Then his hand rested on his heart.

"Can you show us how Jesus can move from up here, to down here, please?"

I saw a deep thirst in his eyes as he pleaded with us.

"Yes, that's why we are here," Kim said.

We led them into prayers of repentance, and the chief and his wife wept as they prayed aloud. After what appeared to be a time of mourning, they began to cup their hands and clap loudly while they rocked back and forth in sudden joy. The chief opened his eyes and said, "We clap because we feel Jesus move from our heads to our hearts, and we are so happy!"

The joy and relief on their faces brought me such deep fulfillment. I thought, *I can do this for the rest of my life!* Suddenly, a look of alarm crossed the face of the chief as he tilted his head to the side. He looked as if he were listening to something that we could not yet hear.

"I think you better climb down our hill right now," he said anxiously. Then he continued very matter-of-factly, "Too late!"

At that moment, sheets of rain plastered the tin roof of the hut, and the structure swayed slightly, surrendering to the winds of the kind of sudden storm the islanders called pineapple showers.

Kim and I jumped to our feet and the chief led us to the door, which he quickly opened so we could survey the landscape. The dark rain clouds had already enveloped the city of Suva, and we couldn't see more than a couple of yards ahead. "Not a good time to go down; you might as well just stay with us."

Kim immediately interjected, "We'd love to, but we have to get back to our team."

"Really?" he asked, as we saw that the trail we had walked up was now a little stream.

"I have an umbrella," Kim said, "We can walk slowly on top of the rocks of the trail, and we should get down just fine." I wasn't so sure.

Nonetheless after saying our warm goodbyes to our new Fijian friends we began the trek, stone by stone, slowly down the hillside, huddled under Kim's umbrella. We were doing very well for a while, and I was proud of us. Though my back was soaked, I managed to keep almost all the rain and oozing mud off Kim. Suddenly, mid-hill, a gust of wind pushed us down, and then pulled so strong on the umbrella that I let go of Kim's shoulder for a moment to save it. Once I stabilized the umbrella, I was shocked to find that Kim was no longer next to me! Where did she go?

I looked down and there she was, sitting in the middle of a pool in front of me, legs in the air and a little waterfall crashing against her back. She had been relying on my shoulder grip for balance, so once I removed it, she slipped off the top of the rocks and landed bottom first into the pool.

Kim yelled, "Don't just stand there, get me out of here!"

I never saw Kim look so vulnerable; I liked it. There she sat, water and mud oozing its way through her hair and over her dress. That's when the tickle in my gut rose. I tried to fight it; I thought of life's more tragic moments, which only made the tickle increase. There on that hillside I couldn't fight it any longer. It was no use. I surrendered to the gut-laugh.

What happens when you surrender to that hard kind of laughter? Your body gets weak—I couldn't get Kim out of the pool! I'd lift her up, and drop her down again. Once I finally got her to her feet, I was so happy to see that she was laughing too. "Thanks for the help," she said sarcastically as she proceeded down the trail and the rains kept saturating the landscape. When we reached a slippery, rockless plain I fell face forward into the mud. Kim cackled as she looked back with a victorious grin. After I peeled myself out of the clay mold my body left in the mud, and realized that the rocky part of the trail was behind I said, "Why should we walk the rest of the way when we can slide?"

And slide we did.

Once we arrived to the bottom of the hill and were laughing at the results of our mud bath, we could hear other laughter off in the distance.

There on top of the hill were all the villagers pointing down at us! And there, in all that laughter, I heard the whisper of the Father say, "My son, I don't want you to leave Fiji until each one of their names are written in my Lamb's Book of Life—bring my missing children home."

In that moment I became acutely aware that I was living in the center of a dream God had for me, and for this village, long before I was born.

I couldn't wait to go back to the hilltop and show the villagers that no storm was going to keep me away from returning. So that night I hiked back up the trail and was immediately greeted with many smiles and giggles. One of the Fijian teenagers said, "We didn't think you'd be coming back after that wipe out!" Seven of the young adult men gathered around me, curious as to why I returned. "I'll explain later," I said, and whipped out two decks of Uno cards. "Does anyone want to play?"

Within two weeks the Uno card games evolved into a Bible study. That Bible study led many of the villagers into their own unique encounters with God.

One Bible study night Marino stood in front of the little community, and in a very straightforward fashion said, "Jeff, you say that God is a loving Father. If that is true, then He knows that I have no job, and my wife's birthday is coming, and I have nothing to give her. So tomorrow I will pray, 'Jeff's God please give me a job right now so I have something nice to get for my wife—and so I know you want to be my Father, too.'"

I didn't know what to say. I returned to my outreach team that evening and in desperation said, "We all have to pray that God gives Marino a job tomorrow, or I don't know what I'm going to say at the Bible study!"

Blessed Are the Pure in Heart

Two mornings later I saw Marino's head bobbing up and down through the kitchen window of our outreach house. He was trying to get my attention during one of our team meetings. I slid out the back door to see what he wanted. In excitement and with a loss of breath he explained to me, "Yesterday I was walking by the sugar mill praying for a job when a man walked out of the mill and immediately looked at me and said, 'Do you need a job? We have an opening that you can fill if you want to start today.' I was speechless, and then said, 'yes, of course, for sure, sir.' Then my eyes filled with tears—not a good thing for a Fijian man. I thought, *Wow, Jeff's Father wants to be my Father; Jeff's God wants to be my God!*"

That night when the rest of the villagers heard the story everyone began to ask God for things and each week there were more testimonies of his provisions and faithfulness. Even though the villagers were new Christians with just a basic understanding of biblical theology, I was overwhelmed to see how God honored the prayers of the childlike in heart.

I'll never forget Simon's story. "I was at math class today," he said, "and my teacher wrote a big equation on the board and said, 'Simon come up and write the answer on the board!' Of course I'm dumb when it comes to math. I didn't know the answer. So I prayed as I walked up, 'Jeff's God, and Marino's God, please give me the answer.' Then I wrote the answer on the board and the teacher and all of the class were very shocked. I said, 'that's not me; that's God!' The teacher replied, 'you're right, that's not you; that has to be God!'"

All the villagers laughed hysterically at Simon's punchline.

As God invaded each of their lives with his love, some of the villagers joined with us in sharing their newfound faith in God with other villagers. On one of these occasions Marino said to me, "You have brought us Jesus and a good Father so we have to give you something in return." Then he turned to his buddies, Villie and Sam, and they began to discuss what they could give me.

"Ah ha, I know what we can give you Jeff, we can teach you spear fishing!" Villie exclaimed. It sounded fun to me.

It wasn't.

They tried to teach me how to spear fish on one breath, like they have been doing since they were eight years old. They couldn't grasp why I couldn't do the same.

"You come up too quickly," Marino sternly explained to me. "You go down this time and *pray harder* that Father God will give you a fish!"

Well it didn't work, and I came up empty-speared again. They were discouraged, and I could hear them mumbling to each other, "Jeff is a bad fisherman huh, how will he ever feed his family?"

"Ok," they said, as they revived their hope with a new plan, "Because this is not working we will teach you cliff jumping!"

Another fun idea—in concept.

However once we hiked through the jungle I saw the reality of the situation: there was a 35-foot drop off a large rock in a very narrow pool. You had to swing out holding onto a vine. If you didn't let go at the right time your body would fall on top of the sharp surrounding rocks—apparently the suspense of that possibility was supposed to be the fun part.

There I stood on the edge of the rock cliff with a dangling vine next to me. With extreme reluctance I stared at the water and rocks below. *This is crazy*, I thought, *what am I about to do? Why give my life away as a missionary to the first country I visit?* But the guys pestered me so much, as they showed me over and over again the right way, and time, to let go of the vine. I finally surrendered. I grabbed the vine, pushed myself away from the rock, and to my shock three of the guys jumped onto the vine with me! I'm sure they doubted my ability to tackle this on my own. I remember feeling the fuzzy hair of one of them beneath me when I hit the water and my fingertips touched the sharp rocks that were on both sides of the pool.

I crawled out of the water, shouting a THANK YOU to God in my mind as I tried to act un-affected and cool. *I made it*, I thought, *without killing myself or anyone else.* I could hear one of my friends quietly mumble to another, "Wow, he almost hit the rocks, he's not good at this either! I guess we can't give him a present after all."

An Unforgettable Evening

I was dreading my last night in Fiji. The village had become my home, and its people my people. The Fijian portion of our outreach was over, and we had a two-week mission in Western Samoa before heading back to Maui, Hawaii, for the DTS graduation.

The villagers were insistent that I spend my last night with them. I remember my sullen walk up the trail as I wondered, *How did these people become such a big part of my heart so quickly?* When I arrived to the top of the trail the sweet and spicy smell of curry, fish and papaya washed over me. Sam placed his hand on my back and led me to my spot as a guest of honor at dinner. My meal was served on a large leaf as villagers danced in the middle of the circle and others put flowers and shell necklaces around my neck. While they performed, gifts were laid in front of me. Then the chief stood up and said, "We will never forget you Jeff. You have given us the greatest gift of all, a loving Father, Jesus, and a wonderful God. Please, please return to us someday."

We talked and laughed for several hours and recounted our favorites stories of my time in Fiji. We determined who were the best cheaters and winners of our killer Uno card games. Not everyone agreed. Then Mario, Sam and Ville dismissed themselves to clear out a large space in the middle of the village. "This is where a bunch of us are going to sleep tonight," they told me as they laid huge wicker mats on the ground, "side by side under the stars." Several of the guys grabbed their pillows and blankets and took their places—they reserved one long, skinny spot for me.

I'm a light sleeper, I thought, *how will I sleep with all these people around me?* Then the chief and his wife, accompanied by the rest of the villagers, gathered in front of us with their ukuleles and began to sing the most harmonious music I've ever heard. I drifted to sleep on the soothing melody.

After about two hours I awoke to music still playing. I leaned forward and was surprised to see that they were still staring at me singing. I said, "It's getting late, go to bed!"

"Tomorrow you are leaving us and our eyes won't see you anymore," they said. "We look at you now and take you through our eyes and into our hearts; there you will always be. So go back to sleep now, Jeff."

I dozed off again and when I opened my eyes, I was shocked again to see the villagers still singing and staring at me! They had stood there all night.

A Painful Goodbye

The bright morning sun reached its golden fingers through the light haze that hung on the hilltop. My breakfast was cooking over the fire, and the sound of its crackling flames only highlighted the stillness of the moment, the absence of words, and the tone of my departure. Marino handed me a fried puff pastry without his usual eye contact and playful grin. It was my time to say goodbye. A couple of miles away my outreach team would be getting ready to leave for the airport, and I needed to catch a bus at the bottom of the hill to join them. I visited every hut with few words and a burning sensation in my throat as I held back tears. Then I began the old familiar trek down the hillside where only weeks before Kim and I had slid so gracefully.

Never had that walk felt so lonely.

At the bottom I heard whistles from off in the distance behind me. There on the hilltop were all the villagers huddled together—some were waving, and others cried as they held each other. In that moment a blanket of warmth and joy fell upon me, and I heard the divine whisper say to me, "Well done, my good and faithful son! Thank you for bringing my missing children home."

I boarded the local bus, overwhelmed by a myriad of emotions. When I arrived to the outreach house and got off the bus, I was shocked to see all the villagers waiting!

"You are making this the hardest goodbye of my life," I said, "and how did you get here so fast?"

"We took short cuts through the backstreets and bush," Sam said. "Where have you been?" the others retorted in glee. "Besides, our eyes can still see you— you haven't left Fiji yet." Marino piped in, "We will help you and everyone pack the bus!"

With much excitement and a great sense of mission, the village men packed our luggage on the bus for the ride to the airport. I went to the very back seat so I could still see everyone and talk with them before we pulled away. Villie's younger brother jumped up to my bus window next to me. Bare-chested, he handed me the only shirt I ever saw him wear. "Last gift for you!" he said.

I took my shirt off and put his on, which didn't even make it down to my navel. Then Marino yelled, "Quickly throw us your brown book before you leave. We want to write in it." They had noticed that with my Bible I always carried my journal so I could transcribe the stories of God and always remember their details. (I thank my Mormon upbringing for that habit.) I tossed my journal to them, and they all huddled around it, writing.

The rumble of the bus engine turning over was our signal that it was time to leave. The men tossed my journal back as we began to pull away from the curb. I opened it up to see what they had written.

On one side of the page were various names and signatures with quick scribbled artwork. On the other side of the page were all the guys' names in a row with military terms next to them: Sergeant Marino, Lieutenant Sam, Captain Villie, etc. At the bottom of the row was the phrase, "We are soldiers for Christ and forever we will stand! Thank you for giving us a Father, for giving us God."

As the bus began to pull away the men lined up in a single file facing me. After Marino gave a signal they all saluted—too smooth to have been done without practice. Then I could barely see anyone through the dust stirred up by the bus and the tears in my eyes.

That moment was sacred. While I had given the villagers my heart they had given me my mission.

Your Story

There is part of your village, city or rural area that is in need of your gift, your personality, and your contribution. There is an adventure awaiting your discovery that will forever change the lives of those you encounter. We will use an ancient way of praying called Lectio Divina that will prepare you for this. It was part of the devotional practice of the Jews in the days of Jesus, and is a way of listening to the texts of Scripture as if we were in a conversation with Christ and he was suggesting the topics of conversation. I'll explain to you this method of prayer and then give you a biblical text to use as a practice.

1. *Moment One:* **Read** the scripture passage for the first time. Listen with the "ears of your heart," trusting the Spirit's guidance. What word, phrase, or sentence stands out to you? Begin to repeat the sentence or word over and over, allowing it to settle deeply in your heart.

2. *Moment Two:* **Reflect** and relish the words. Let them resound in your heart. Let an attitude of quiet receptiveness permeate the prayer time. What is God saying to you through the text?

3. *Moment Three:* **Respond** spontaneously as you continue to listen to a phrase, sentence or word. A prayer of praise, thanksgiving, or petition may arise. Offer that prayer and consider what you want to say to God about the text.

4. *Moment Four:* **Action.** What do you want to do based on your prayer? Prayer should move us to action. This action may simply be to rest in God and simply "be with Him," or it may prompt you to act on the behalf of another, ask someone for forgiveness, or return to the Scripture allowing the Spirit to help you imagine yourself in the story with Jesus.

Use this portion of scripture portion for your own practice:

"The Spirit of the Lord is on me, because he has anointed me to proclaim good news to the poor. He has sent me to proclaim freedom for the prisoners and recovery of sight for the blind, to set the oppressed free, to proclaim the year of the Lord's favor" (Luke 4:18).

Notes

"God utters me like a word
that contains a partial thought
of Himself."

- *Thomas Merton, Meditation with Merton*

9

Intimacy in Action

"Home is the place where you become yourself," said Pico Iyer.[33] The love of my parents gave me the freedom to choose who I wanted to become, and my Fiji experience showed me that in many ways I was already that person. I didn't need to fall prey any longer to a culture that favors image over reality and having over being. In the Fijian village I felt at home with just a sulu wrapped around my waist, flip-flops, and a tee-shirt. Life was uncluttered; I lived without being ambushed by the *tyranny of the urgent* or the pressures of performance. Space opened in my heart to love deeply. Never had I felt so alive.

Now that my Discipleship Training School is over, I thought, *what should I do? Where should I go?* Corrie Ten Boom's words, "Never be afraid to trust an unknown future with a known God," comforted me. In my Discipleship Training School I had found God to be lovingly knowable, and I felt I could now trust Him with the unknowns of my future. Yet I had a deeper desire than my yearning to know God; I wanted to make Him happy.

Through his extravagant love, God has given us the honor of being able to know Him, I thought, *so how can I give something beautiful back to Him in return?* I thought of Mary's act of devotion when she broke the alabaster box on the feet of Jesus—some have speculated that it was her dowry—and yet serveral of the disciples thought her extravagance was a waste, saying it could have been used for the poor. Jesus responded to His questioning disciples by saying, "Why are you bothering her? She has done a beautiful thing to me" (Mark 14:6)? *How could I accomplish that?*

I began to consider, *who in the world makes God happy?* The first modern contemplative activist that came to mind was Mother Teresa. I read that she woke at 4:00 am in Calcutta, India, with the nuns of her order, and they gathered in a plain white chapel. On the wall hung a crucifix with the words *I thirst*. A bell rang and in spotless white saris the nuns knelt and said in unison, "Let us bless the Lord." After their morning time of adoration they served amongst the poorest of the poor. Their desire was to prevent any person from dying alone.

This must make God happy, I thought. *How could I be equally intimate with Him and mobilized to action,* I wondered? Should I be a teacher, a writer, or a missionary in the foreign field? Mother Teresa's words settled my heart, "Do not worry about your career. Concern yourself with your vocation, and that is to be lovers of Jesus."[34] I could spend my hours and my days learning to do that well.

To embrace this vocation I knew I needed to work with God to form a characteristic in myself that I lacked—the ability to love instinctively—what I had seen to be the highest form of freedom. I didn't want to fall again into the same performance traps and the false self that I'd fashioned before the DTS. I wanted to be free to love others and to make my God happy.

The director of the Maui Youth With A Mission center met with me before graduation and asked me to pray about joining his staff. This would entail leading a mobile team around the States and Canada in the summer, and then returning to Maui to lead a Discipleship Training School. *What a great place to learn leadership skills and how to be a lover of Jesus, I thought. Just maybe I'd learn how to surf and spearfish, too!*

A two-year commitment to a staff position with YWAM-Maui seemed to be the natural next step and a great incubator for my spiritual growth. With Brother Lawrence's book *Practicing the Presence of God* in one hand, and a worn, spongy boogie board in the other, I began the journey of making my home in Youth With A Mission, Maui Hawaii.

The Crucible of Experience

After completing staff training, my first assignment was to lead a team to the Philippines and Hong Kong. Waves of excitement and insecurity flooded me. God was entrusting me with this mission. But would people follow me?

I've led many mission trips since that first experience in Asia but few with such a conscious, utter dependency on God. And though I never considered contemplation and activism within the Christian life, on that mission outreach to the Philippines and Hong Kong, those took shape. I began the trip by imaging what a team of twenty-three young people in the Subic Bay area of the Philippines for two months could accomplish by using Hudson Taylor's words as a template for ministry: "Bear not a single care thyself, one is too much for thee. The work is mine and mine alone, thy work is to rest in Me." [35]

I was hardly in a *resting-in-God* mode when we left Maui to begin our trek to Asia on the Christmas Eve of 1986. There were a handful of students who were not able to join us on our mission because of a lack of financial provision. So what was supposed to be a joyful send-off at the airport became a tear-fest of goodbyes. *Great start*, I remember thinking.

When we arrived at the Honolulu airport to catch our flights to Manila, another disappointment awaited us. We were bumped. "Your group cannot fly out till tomorrow," an airline representative told me.

A rush of anxiety and an invasion of worrisome thoughts overtook me. However, I realized that one of the beautiful gifts God gave us is that we can multi-task, but we can't multi-think. Immediately I started rearranging the inner dialogue of my mind into a contemplative conversation with God, as Brother Lawrence suggests.

This is Your team, I reminded the Lord in my mind, *Your work and mission, not mine. You know what is best, good Father, so I return to my place of abiding peace in You.* In that moment I acknowledged my false self who desired to be a great, in-control leader. I reminded myself of my main vocation—to be a lover of Jesus, which meant I couldn't be a lover of myself; my ego and reputation had to go. Once I made that mental transaction, waves of peace enveloped me.

My team ended up in a hotel with a $200 reimbursement to each person for the inconvenience. We pooled the money, and to our amazement found it was exactly the amount needed for the folks we'd left behind in Maui to join us later on our mission trip!

We arrived at Manila on Christmas Day singing the Hawaiian Christmas carol *Mele Kalikimaka* as we loaded our luggage from the airport into a bus that was going to take us on a three-and-a-half-hour drive to Subic Bay. While pulling out of the station our senses were immediately assaulted by a culture we would learn to embrace as our home for six weeks. Michael Jackson's "Thriller" pulsed in the marketplace, and a unique mixture of exhaust fumes and Asian spices permeated the air. Conventional and unconventional means of public transportation swirled around us. There were war-torn motorcycles with connecting passenger seats, flamboyantly decorated extended Jeeps with Catholic Icons and swinging tassels hanging from rearview mirrors. People squeezed out of everything. We were held in a trance with the circus-like quality of it all while we followed the garbage-littered highway to our destination.

During our orientation to mission work in the Subic Bay area, we were told that because of the strong presence of the US Naval base, there were between twelve and fifteen thousand prostitutes inhabiting the town. We were reminded of this as we drove through this district in several of the extended Jeeps, called Jeepneys, as girls bent over the balconies of the glitzy brothels waving at us and lifting up their shirts.

We arrived at our accommodations about fifteen minutes from the red light district. It was a large concrete structure alongside a bay. If you squinted your eyes, it was pretty with its palm trees waving in the breeze pointing towards the mountains across the gulf. A full on gaze, though, revealed that we were on the edge of a squatters' zone, with garbage and sewage in the stream next to our guesthouse. Nonetheless, we moved in happily on that long Christmas Day, and after taking refreshing bucket showers, we unpacked and made ourselves at home.

Once the lights were extinguished that night, and the team had collapsed in their beds, I stared at a gecko on the ceiling above my bunk, and thought, *We're finally here Father. Now, what is most important to You?* I paused, thought, and listened; the two great commandments came to mind. *We can't go wrong if we make space to love God and each other with all of our hearts*, I thought.

For the next couple of weeks we established a community rhythm where, after breakfast, we dispersed and found our own quiet place— with the distant Jeepney's beeps as background music. In that space we tended to our own hearts, learning to love and be loved by God. This was followed by corporate worship and ensuring our relationships with each other were intact and without offense. "Will we stand in naked truth," Brennan Manning questioned, "or be clothed in fantasy?" That was our challenge as we learned how to walk in truth with each other. Then we waited on God to reveal His purposes and dreams for Subic Bay. That was our unremarkable, simple community rhythm, framed by the two great commandments.

Our first corporate prayer times consisted of asking God, *What is our mission in this place? What are You already doing that You are inviting us to be part of?* A church we attended one Sunday told us that they had prayed for 25 years for missionaries to come to Subic Bay and to see the stronghold of prostitution broken. During our time of waiting on God, several of the students felt the words *honor, respect,* and *dignity* come to mind, accompanied by a sense of compassion for the women in the brothels. We asked each other, *How could these impressions give birth to a strategy to help these girls?* An idea emerged. "Let's have the men dress up in nice formal clothes," one of the girls said, "and with roses in hand enter the brothels and invite each of the girls to come to a Bible study that we host!"

"That would be awesome," one of the guys, piped in. "We will be treating the women with the honor and respect that they probably never had."

The room erupted with excitement. Within a couple of days the vision was put into place and our men headed into the red light district, leaving a trail of various cologne scents behind them. As was predicted, the ladies in the brothels were deeply touched by the respectful invitation.

"You don't want anything from us," one of the girls asked a small group of our men, rather perplexed?

"Nothing at all," one of them responded, "though we would like you to consider joining us for an evening of learning about God and how He feels about you."

That evening all the benches in our meeting room were packed with women from the brothels. As we shared the gospel and challenged the girls to leave their lifestyles and become Christ-followers, tears began to leave tiny trails of makeup down many of their faces. Two of the ladies boldly stood up and began praying out loud, surrendering their lives to the Lover of their souls. The next week our Bible Study was so filled that the large room could not fit another person. Outside the windows you could see both ladies and men leaning through the barred windows, thirsty to hear about God's unrelenting passion for them, and His dream to *make all things new.* That evening, two new Christian ladies shared their newfound faith, pleading with the girls to come follow Jesus, and over half of the room responded.

Our first two disciples wanted to immediately leave their brothels but were held by a large financial debt. During a corporate prayer time several students challenged us to put financial feet to our own prayers by taking up an offering. After quieting our hearts we passed around an empty, rusty dishpan. Joyful anticipation was like an electrical current in the room. The offering was counted and it totaled the exact amount needed for the girls to be released!

The weeks that followed these events spurred a revival in the region, not only amongst the prostitutes but also among those addicted to drugs, those in marriages on the verge of collapse, and those who were lonely and broken—all those who were vulnerable enough to acknowledge a need for a Savior. This was the first time in my life in which I saw how God blesses a unified people. Our goal had been to love God and each other well and to be a people of action. In the Philippines, I saw how God rides in on the actions of His people. If there are no actions, there is no blessing. If the Israelites hadn't walked around Jericho, the walls would never have come tumbling done. As Richard Rohr says, "Contemplation is not the opposite of action; it's the opposite of reaction." [36]

During our Philippine mission, I sat on a beach in Subic Bay after we baptized a long line of people. My friend Bill played worship music and everyone sang. I realized how private my spirituality was. Now I saw very clearly how God's primary interest was not in my sweet little relationship with Him. I realized He is in search of a people, like He was in his pursuit of Israel—a people He could bless. Looking at the faces of those around me singing and laughing, I thought, *This is it!* Scripture teaches how we are known to be His disciples by our love for one another, not only by our love for God.

Thoughts of God

"God utters me like a word that contains a partial thought of Himself," [37] Thomas Merton said, and I've grown into the understanding of this statement over the course of my life. This statement suggests that I don't have to be the entirety of God's thoughts to the world—what a relief. I only need to live out my small piece. When we live this out together in the context of community, we become a mosaic picture of the face of Jesus to the world.

But this begs the question: What God thoughts do I embody, and what is my place in the missional mosaic? Ever since my teen years my Mormon friends said I carried a sense of peace. When I became a Christian, church members gave me tasseled bookmarkers describing the meaning of my name—*the divinely peaceful one.* How boring, I thought. Why couldn't my name mean something like Mighty Prince of Valor? I have a dear friend named Brenda Lewis. When she walks into a room she brings such a sense of life, laughter and fun. I used to think, *why couldn't I be that?* I have another friend who, when he preaches, he powerfully energizes the crowd to conviction and action. When I preach I make people cry.

It has taken me a long time to love and celebrate the person God has made me to be and to fully own the thoughts of God I carry. The voice that has called out God's idea of me, when I could not see it myself, has been the voice of authentic community.

I've learned to live into this sense of peace only by connection with community.

Twenty-one years after my mission trip to the Philippines, in the early winter of 2007 I arrived at the San Diego airport after teaching in Ensenada, Mexico. While looking for my connecting flight I glanced up at a TV monitor and was struck by an oddly familiar image on CNN. There were the grounds of a YWAM base in Arvada, Colorado, where I often teach. Under the picture words scrolled by that read, "Early this morning an unidentified man with a pistol opened fire at a Youth With A Mission center killing one person and wounding two others before escaping: investigation in progress."

I turned my phone on, and loads of messages from the Denver area bombarded my screen. One of my texts read: "Jeff, I'm sorry. It looks like your buddy Dan is critically injured and has a bullet stuck in his throat, and I don't think that his girlfriend Tiffany is going to make it."

I gasped as a sudden rush of air hit the back of my throat. I had just given Dan and Tiffany a blessing on their budding romantic relationship three months ago. Though my teaching schedule for the next two weeks was full, there was no doubt what I had to do. I immediately rearranged my schedule and flew into Denver a day later.

After getting settled in my guest room, I tuned in to the story. After the shootings, the perpetrator, Matthew Murray, killed two more people in Colorado Springs before being shot and wounded by a member of the New Life Church he had attacked. He then committed suicide. I also received a text and learned that Tiffany had already passed away. Dan was heavily sedated, the text read, and was in immense pain. Unsettled, I drove to the hospital to see Dan.

When I stepped into his room, he was propped up against a pile of pillows and huge bandages were wrapped around his throat. He mumbled once our eyes connected, "Hey Jeff," then paused as a wave of emotion made it impossible for him to speak. I walked over to him and put one of my arms around his shoulders and leaned my head against his. I remember thinking, *it seemed like only yesterday he and Tiffany were so full of the life young love brings.* Once his body stopped trembling he let out a sigh of relief and whispered, "Let's go see Tiff; let's make sure she is O.K."

For a moment I didn't know how to respond.

"I think it's better that you just stay here and rest a while, Dan."

"Ok," he said. We were silent for a moment as I sat down.

"I'm starting to get better now," he said.

"Really?" I exclaimed, still struck by the size of the bandages around his neck.

"Yes," he said, shifting a bit in the pillows, "When you walked into the room and I saw your face, I relaxed; I knew *Peace* is here and everything is going to be okay."

The next 48 hours Dan came in and out of the awareness of

Tiffany's death, as hundreds of visitors arrived to offer their condolences and to be present with their friend. Amongst the chaos I witnessed again the dynamism of the abiding life lived out in community. In that hospital room, among the community of faith, there was a stillness into which the world cannot intrude, an ancient peace that no fire of calamity could extinguish. Though I was wrecked by the pain of what had happened, I also experienced the fulfillment of embracing God's idea of me—the joy of being an ambassador of peace. I also experienced the community, working in concert to show the love of Christ to a wounded man.

This tragedy has marked many lives, but so has the response of those involved—the victims, the local community, and the international outpouring of love. The Murrays expressed their profoundly broken and repentant hearts to the parents of the victims for what their son had done. Forgiveness, hope and healing were extended instead of hatred, revenge and bitterness.

A Peaceful Revolution

When you and I know the thoughts of God we embody, and carry them where they are most needed in the world—whether to the Philippines, Colorado Springs, or the neighbor next door—we have discovered our activism. As we walk this out within an authentic community that practices the presence of God and joins Him in His activity, we become part of a powerful global force of Christ-followers. And the character of that force is not marked by what we are against, but in the tenacious quality of our love—knowing that the best criticism of the bad is the practice of the better. [38] This could be the peaceful revolution that surprises the world.

Your Story

John 15 is the sacred text where intimacy and action are so beautifully entwined. We are challenged to *abide and remain in God's love*, which results in meaningful service, producing *fruit that will last*. Through two reflective exercises let's discover how we can accomplish this by becoming our authentic selves.

1. Read John 15:1-17 slowly, giving time for God to speak. What is He showing you regarding the abiding life?

2. In your journal write down the consistent compliments you have received from others over the years, regarding your character and personality.

Translate the above compliment list into *thoughts of God*. How can you consistently give them away to the world?

Notes

"The things we see are but the shadows created by the things we don't see."

- Martin Luther King Jr.

10
Everlasting Walls?

The dark shadow of Haleakala Volcano emerged as our plane descended over sugarcane fields and onto the airstrip of the Kahului Airport in Maui, Hawaii. After three months in the Philippines and Hong Kong, the students felt as if they were returning to their home away from home; I simply felt I was returning home. A mission vocation was now my chosen life—somehow it had adopted me. The students would be leaving in a week after celebrating the completion of their Discipleship Training School. I would remain another two months and finish my staff commitment to YWAM Maui before investigating other mission opportunities.

Twenty-four years old and a career choice made, I felt it was a perfect time for God to give me a life partner, the "One" to serve alongside me. I thought surely *the one* would have abilities to complement mine so that we could be the total ministry package to the world. She'd be administrative because I thought those kinds of things were boring but needful. She'd also need to become best friends immediately with my parents—particularly my mom—Dad would like anyone I chose as a wife. And maybe most importantly, she'd need to be the kind of girl whose beauty and God-ward love would make all my brothers jealous. But where was she?

The Mormon way of finding a spouse seemed much easier—the returning missionary male was a hot commodity. In the Christian mission field though, many were already married, and I often had to weed through slim pickings. Mom didn't help me out either. She was nice and accommodating to the girls I brought her way in that formal sort of way, but I don't think she thought any of them were good enough for me. I didn't either; I'm ashamed to say it. I was way too picky and had a stubborn mind-set and poor relationship theology. Where did I get it in my mind there was just *the one* out there anyway? And though I enjoyed a few healthy romantic relationships, I couldn't make the marriage commitment. I missed out on many gals I'm sure would have made exceptional wives and mothers.

Mindsets often determine the choices we make and the direction of our futures. In those days, I had a growing relationship with God but several blind spots in the way I saw relationships and the role of the mind in Christian spirituality. I viewed Christianity as a matter of the heart and not of the mind. I believed that so long as I didn't think evil or lustful thoughts about others and so long as I pondered the things of God, I was being faithful. Since then I've come to agree with the Dali Lama, "A change of heart must lead to a change of mind." If one's mind doesn't change, nothing will change.

In my mid to late twenties I had a consistent prayer life, but I didn't understand the process of mind renewal—the only practice that makes long-term change and an ability to discern God's perfect will possible. Too often I neglected the discipline of marinating in truth long enough for it to transform me. I preferred the spiritual high of new revelation, the new book, teaching, and seminar. I was a consumer of truth instead of its practitioner. And these consumptive ways didn't allow for a change of heart or mind. I had a mind-set that God was going to provide a perfect mate for me, and yet I feared being controlled by women.

Contemplation sifts us into stillness so we can have a growing relationship with God's truth as a heart and mind experience. And until that happens, truth will only bounce off our stony hearts, or otherwise embitter us instead of setting us free. I've learned through contemplative practice to become a detective of my mind so that I can see people—particularly women—differently. Now, I don't assume any women should be my perfect complement or might otherwise seek to control me. Contemplation enables me to slow down and see others for who they are. Contemplation of the ways in which Christ sees me allows me to see others through the eyes of the Crucified instead of through the lens of my dysfunctions, fractures, and fears.

My Parent's Mantra

Tim, the fourth born son, was the first to get married. Initially this was surprising because I had been the kid with all the crushes, and I was the perpetual romantic. But I was proud of Tim, and I loved his fiancé Becky, a close friend of our family. Tim and Becky had both attended the Discipleship Training Schools I led, and they both wanted to follow and serve God. But responsibility and commitment were not words I associated with Tim.

Tim was the most challenging and emotional of all us kids, and we all figured he'd never be ready for marriage—marriage would have to make him ready. Until that happened we assumed Tim and Becky's hormones and good looks would have to carry them for a while. And they did.

Marriage and missions were my parent's hopeful mantra for us kids. Within the course of a decade, not only did Tim and Becky take a DTS and get married, but so did the rest of the Dream team—Reid first, then Lee, then Nicole. All of them went to separate DTS programs and married shortly after. And though I felt I had been ready for marriage during my three years with YWAM Maui, my unhealthy mindsets were like a wall around my heart that stifled my emotions. I had been too emotionally available as a teenager. (Remember the ring from Target I gave to Christine when I was 14?) Now I was too guarded. And in pursuit of *the abiding life*, as I mentioned in the last chapter, I had a tendency to over-spiritualize things. I remember asking one love interest in Maui, "How can I have feelings for you and love God with all of my heart, mind and strength?" I couldn't understand yet that loving others is akin to loving God, and that the most magnificent gift we can give the world is loving a wife as Christ loved the church.

Adventures with Mercy Ships

During my years in Maui, I kept current with the journeys of the flagship of Mercy Ships, the *Anastasis*. When I made my first public declaration of my call to missions at Keith Green's Memorial Concert, I was initially exposed to the ministry of Mercy Ships. I connected with its vision to carry the "two-handed gospel"— ministering to both the physical and spiritual needs of people. With a few years of mission experience behind me, I thought Mercy Ships might provide the next step in my experience of the needs of the world. At the time it was docked in Victoria, on Vancouver Island, British Columbia, Canada, a couple of hours from my parents on Whidbey Island. I would join the ministry at a perfect time, when the ship's long dry-dock was ending and it was preparing to sail down the west coast of the States to minister in Mexico.

Throughout my time with YWAM in Maui, I felt the organization was well-intentioned but unprofessional. At that time, Mercy Ships was part of YWAM, but I should have known that managing ocean-going disaster relief ships required a measure of professionalism. Mercy Ships was the Christian counterpart to the many Mormon ministries with which I worked, minus the suits and ties. I immediately felt comfortable with its efficiency because it seemed familiar.

I came to YWAM with a rehearsed, formal version of myself—even my hair was always perfectly manicured. But YWAM Maui helped loosen me up. During my first year with Mercy Ships, the professionalism and skilled staff created a fertile ground for me to fall prey again to my insecurities and performance orientation. But once I saw the ways in which I tried to show myself accomplished and put together—once I noticed the reemergence of my false self—I shifted my attention from trying to be the capable administrative person Mercy Ships valued to reminding myself of the smile of the One who was most important to me. "How can I live for His pleasure," became the cry of my heart once again.

During my mid to late twenties, while in service with Mercy Ships, I often wondered about my niche in ministry. I knew I was a carrier of peace, but I desired more clarity about my activism. I wondered how my life could produce lasting change for the sake of the gospel. Then, while studying aboard the ship, I was struck by this statement made by Irenaeus: "The Glory of God is man fully alive." At first I thought, *What a narcissistic statement; what does God's glory have to do with my aliveness?* This inner question was suddenly interrupted by Jesus' words; "I have come to give you life, and life to the full." Could it be that God's glory was wrapped up in my enjoyment of my God-given and unearned uniqueness, in giving myself to others as I served as a missionary? This sounded too simple.

But then I considered another question. *Is our greatest witness to a watching world to be a people who are fully alive?* This prompted me to write a list of things that made me come alive. It began with *hiking in the wilderness*, and ended with *seeing an orphaned child have a home*. And as I expounded upon the list, I wrote "running when I'm in shape" and then remembered one of my heroes of my early twenties, Eric Liddell.

Eric Liddell was an Olympic runner who received much notoriety for not competing on Sunday because of his religious convictions. He also received some ridicule from his sister for not giving up running to be a missionary in China, which she saw as his more spiritual calling. In the movie about his life entitled *Chariots of Fire*, there's a beautiful scene where his sister challenges what she perceives to be his secular aspiration. Lidell responded, "Jennie I am going to be a missionary in China. God has made me for a purpose, for China, but He has also made me fast. When I run I feel His pleasure." Lidell's statement settled my heart. I was heading in the right direction in my journey of making my God happy. He is glorified as I experience fullness of life, and as I find Him in all things, with no secular and sacred divide—no wall between.

A Vision For Europe

During my three years of living on the *Anastasis* I led a three-month DTS lecture phase program, and afterwards, a two-month mission outreach to the countries where the ship might dock. After being off ship I loved returning to my little thirty-square-foot room aboard. It was the first home I had where the back yard would change every couple of weeks. If you didn't like the view, you'd simply wait until the next port. I relished the fact that by stepping out of my cabin, I could interact with people of thirty-five different nationalities, and a 423-person crew full of purpose. I loved the everyday drama of nautical life, and the fact that all of our daily needs could be met within a short fifteen-minute walk. If I woke up in the night hungry, I could venture to a part of the ship where the South Pacific island guys lived— they were always eating. If I needed a haircut, fun friends, or mischief, they were just a couple of staircases away.

There was one DTS in which I especially connected with a few of the students—we belonged to each other quickly and so did our dreams. We all carried a fascination for Europe and a vision to reintroduce its nations to the warmth of a personal God.

Among my new friends and fellow visionaries was an eloquent, prophetic young man named Johnny Sertin from England, and a beautiful Kiwi couple, James and Susan Wearne. In the late evening hours, on the tropical island of Grenada in the Caribbean, we'd conspire and scheme about accomplishing our evangelical invasion of Europe while visiting all its most intriguing places. We felt our vision could mutually benefit Mercy Ships because they were going to send the *Anastasis* back to Europe, where she hadn't visited for over a decade. We imagined ourselves serving Mercy Ships as a pre-advance team, visiting the ports where the *Anastasis* would dock.

Once our outreach was over in Grenada, we returned to the ship and I was honored to have the Founder and President of Mercy Ships, Don Stephens, approve our vision for a European ministry team. Within a couple of months we gathered together a nine-member group that included a Fijian, a Tongan, another Brit and two more Americans, one of them being my brother Reid. We gathered at a YWAM base in Harpendon, England, and spent a month preparing for our six-month journey.

Making Spiritual History

At the beginning of our European tour, during our time in Harpendon, England, encouraging words were given to us about how we were to expect God to use us. One said, "Your message will be like a crack in a spiritual wall around the nations, and it will open the eyes of those who are blind to how God feels about them. Your message will revolutionize the hearts of many." I remember thinking, occasional skeptic as I was, *nice words, but it seems a bit overstated and exaggerated.* But another staff member had a similar word, drawing his reference from Joshua 6:20, which read, "When the people gave a loud shout, the wall collapsed; so every man charged straight in, and they took the city."

In Europe, our main tool of ministry became a dramatic presentation that we produced called, "The Bride," which conveyed God's relentless pursuit of us amongst the everyday vices that warred for the affections of our hearts. We felt that with the interest in Christianity at an all-time low in Europe, people needed to see the utter vulnerability of a God who is affected by our infidelities, and yet is painfully waiting to restore and redeem the beloved of His heart. There was another hope I carried in my heart as I created this production; my secret prayer was *God as I care for your Bride may you also care for mine.*

One performance on the streets of Glasgow, Scotland, is etched into my memory. The production was more than half over, and the bridegroom's gaze was transfixed upon the bride. Visible pain furrowed his brow as he watched the bride become wounded, tarnished, and broken under the weight of her entrapments. The music of her belovedness to God began to play, and as she glanced at the ring on her finger, she remembered the love that is better than life, a love that will not let her go. The bridegroom stepped forward and in agony began to dance alone, remembering the days he was intimate with his bride.

It was during this scene on the streets of Glasgow that a black-leathered biker turned the street corner, revving his engine so loudly that it echoed across the old city plaza. To our amazement he abruptly brought his bike to a halt and removed his helmet, his eyes riveted on our production. After its final scene he stood there, frozen. His face held the expression of a troubled, humbled man.

Johnny walked up to him and asked, "Are you okay?"

"No I'm not, "he responded. "My eyes have caught the look of God, and I see how lonely He is for me. Many years ago I knew Him; we were close. But I left Him for the things of the world and never thought He would want me back."

Watching this man come home to God that day was the joy we experienced time and again throughout Western Europe and the European Eastern Block. The dynamics I had witnessed with my team in the Philippines and Hong Kong were evident again: we were a community rich in love for God and each other, conveying His passionate desire to have our hearts, and the hearts of the world.

Many months into the tour, after England and Scotland, after Czechoslovakia and Poland, we were driving back to Berlin when, to our shock, hundreds of cars were exiting Germany, passing us on the other side of the road. *What had happened in Germany*, we wondered, knowing that we had been away from global news for two weeks? At the border crossing, the security attendant had a bottle of Vodka in his hand and a wild look of excitement in his eyes. He noticed our questioning expressions and proclaimed with jubilant force, "The wall has come down! Germany is now one nation!" We were shocked; two weeks ago there hadn't been any hints of this extraordinary event.

We picked up our pace and drove into East Berlin and bought a few chisels and hammers. We drove directly to the Berlin Wall to get a piece of freedom. We found an area of the wall where a colorful spray-painted statement was plastered across the cement, "Walls are not everlasting!" They had come down, just like in Joshua's days.

Two weeks before, the Iron Curtain had looked so ominous and austere. Now people were sitting on it in colorful hoodies, hooting and hollering. Before our eyes was a structure that men had cried against and died against—now it was treated as a thing to be torn down, even a plaything to be enjoyed. Such is the final verdict of the madness of all manmade constructs and mindsets that exclude, divide and elevate. As Martin Luther said, "The things we see are but the shadows created by the things we don't see." [39]

Crouching before the crumbling wall with my friend Johnny, we entered a prophetic moment—history was not only being made in the world but also in our lives. Just as Johnny chipped away diligently at the concrete structure until a piece finally gave way, there would be a day that he would chip away at the constructs of religiosity around England and abroad. And as I lived out my God story in the years ahead, I would use this moment as an illustration, and it would illuminate the walls around the hearts of others.

To a contemplative, everything physical carries the symbolism of a redemptive reality. Why is this the case? Because the Risen One has already come, and He is fulfilling His mission to *make all things new,* and now is the time for the Bride to make herself ready, spiritually. Therefore as contemplative Christ-followers our challenge is to "fix our eyes not on what is seen but what is unseen. For what is seen is temporary, but what is unseen is eternal" (1 Cor. 4:18).

Your Story

There are many barriers that prevent us from becoming who we were born to be and to the discovery of our activism—our unique way of reflecting the love of God to the world. I will lead you through several thoughts and questions to help you overcome these barriers that are often in our minds and to release you into the enjoyment of what makes you fully come alive.

1. Meditate on Romans 12: 2 and discern which pattern of this world is most dominant in your thought life: hopelessness, faithless thoughts or unbelief, consistent clutter and distractions, negativity, narcissism (obsessive self-talk), or unhealthy sexual thoughts.

2. Commit to mind renewal through meditating on the truth of the Bible that is contrary to the worldly pattern of your struggle. "If you hold to my teachings you are my disciples, and you will know the truth and the truth will set you free" (John 8:31, 32). This means that if we continue in, tarry in, abide in, and linger with the truth—then, and only then—we will be set free.

3. Write down your *Alive List*, those things you do in which you sense God's pleasure and a deep sense of aliveness and fulfillment. How are you going to carve out space for this list to be part of your life and your contribution to the world?

"Sow a thought and you reap an action
Sow and action and you reap a habit,
Sow a habit and you reap a character,
Sow a character and you reap a destiny."
-Charles Reed [40]

Notes

"We are not necessarily doubting that God will do the best for me; we are wondering how painful the best will turn out to be."

- C.S. Lewis

11

Treasures of Darkness

The followers of Jesus who have marked my life are those who have endured great hardship, pain, or loss and have somehow become richer, deeper, and more compassionate people because of it. And though my journey had been relatively pain-free well into my twenties, that was about to change.

Shortly after my European travels several friends felt impressed to give me Isaiah 45:3: "I will give you treasures of darkness, riches stored in secret places that you will know I am the Lord your God, the one who summons you by name." I pondered this verse and considered that its reference was to the life-transforming truths not easily found by casual enquirers of God, but truths reserved for desperate seekers—those who are diligent through hard seasons of trial, suffering, and pain.

For six months I was in a long distance secret relationship with a woman who was from Melbourne, Australia. It was secret because her parents only wanted her to marry a doctor (she was a nurse), and I wanted to surprise my family and friends by bringing home "The One," my future wife—already engaged.

Her name was Rosalyn and I met her in Los Angeles between two short-term mission trips while visiting a friend. She was on a break from practicing nursing with Mother Teresa's ministry in Calcutta, India. She had been deeply impacted by the nuns she was working with and was taking some time out to consider if becoming a nun was her destiny. I had another plan for her life.

Rosalyn and I dreamed of going to Italy someday; that was our original connecting point. I was the only man she knew who liked the very dated movie entitled *Brother Sun, Sister Moon*, made in Italy in 1972; it was the story of the early years of St. Francis. While capturing the simplicity of Francis's faith in God and love for creation, the movie also depicted Francis's intense spiritual union with Clare. I was convinced that God was going to give me a similar experience with Rosalyn.

It was not to be. Rosalyn had sugar diabetes and struggled with her health. She became infected with a virus while she was in Calcutta. She was transported back to a hospital in Los Angeles for special treatment. Within the course of six weeks, while receiving medical care, she passed away.

I was heartbroken. An unfamiliar anguish ravished my soul. *God how could this happen to me,* I wondered? I carried this pain as a tormentor until I joined a seafood processor in the Bering Sea of Alaska. There, I learned a most valuable lesson about the treasures of darkness.

Escapism to an Alaskan Seafood Processor

The Aleutian Islands off the coast of Alaska were remote compared to any other place I had been in the world. When a job opened up for me there, it held a certain appeal. After the loss of my love, I needed to find my true north: my spiritual bearings again. I could sense the callback to abide though I still hungered for a love more tangible than God's seemed to be at the time.

I prayed, *God may I somehow find You in this new job. May I hear*

Your voice again. I prayed for the new roommates I would live with, and with a calm excitement I took a car, plane, taxi, and ferry to Dutch Harbor, Alaska, and boarded a ship called the *Omnisea. This will be old hat,* I thought as I stepped off the gangway. I was familiar with boat life but was looking forward to being paid.

The chief purser led me to my room and knocked on the door. No answer. He turned the knob and pushed, and still it wouldn't open until he pressed his body weight against it. The door finally gave way as billows of smoke rolled into the hallway, and we could hear beer cans and whiskey bottles slide across the floor. Hesitantly I stepped into the room with my luggage in hand, and as the smoke dissipated, I began to see what would become my home for several months. I couldn't rest my eyes anywhere because the walls and ceiling were filled with hard-core pornography; women's body parts were cut out of magazines and taped side by side. I turned and looked directly into the faces of my two roommates who were sitting on one of the two bunk beds. One older man on the bottom bunk looked at me with a toothless grin, his eyes glazed over. He had a pencil thin wispy grey beard that hung down to his navel (he would occasionally get the froth of his coffee and pieces of food caught in its stringy hairs). I would later nickname him "Rip" because he reminded me of what I imagined the fabled character of Rip Van Winkle to look like. A few weeks later, some of us talked late at night about how we would like to cut Rip's stringy, dangling beard off while he was sleeping, but we feared his wrath—he claimed to have killed a man.

My other roommate was sitting on the bunk right above Rip and was snickering as he stared hypnotically into the small screen of a video camera. Curious as to what kept him riveted on the screen and not acknowledging my arrival, I glanced at what he was watching. It was an illegal film that exploited children. Upon seeing the images, I was so jarred and sickened I swayed backward for a moment, on sensory overload. *How could this be,* I wondered, internally frozen in

shock, *a crazy look of delight on the face of this man in the presence
of such unjust horror?* The hell-bent darkness that had bombarded me
sent me reeling. *What am I doing here?* I thought. *Have I made a
mistake in coming?*

Both my roommates were ex-convicts. They had been in and out
of prisons much of their lives, but because they were such hard workers,
a fishing boat or seafood processor would always re-hire them.

Stunned, I put my luggage under one of the beds and climbed onto
my top bunk. *How am I going to sleep in this little den of hell,* I thought
as I peeled the pornography off the ceiling above me. I put my shoulder bag, which had all my important documents—my Bible, journal,
and study materials—safely next to my pillow. Then I lay down,
wanting to relax in an environment that was very foreign to me and
to face the fact that this experience was going to be very different from
living on the Christian love boat of Mercy Ships. As I paused in the
stillness of the moment and someone turned the lights off, I asked God
for his opinion on things. A quote by C.S. Lewis suddenly came to
mind: "We are not necessarily doubting that God will do the best for
me; we are wondering how painful the best will turn out to be." [41]
Could it be that this place, these people, are God's best for me, I
thought, *even though I'm very uncomfortable and in emotional pain?*

Before dozing off, I remembered that I needed to complete some
paperwork for an Old Testament survey correspondent course I was
taking to become ordained. In the morning we would sail from Dutch
Harbor, so I had to get my studies ready to be mailed. I reached for
my flashlight pen and began taking my studies out of my shoulder bag.
The light had only been turned off for a couple minutes when the door
of the room slowly opened, shedding a beam of light across the littered
floor. *It is Jesus,* I thought. I was disappointed.

The silhouette of a woman proceeded to the bunk next to me. When
she unintentionally crunched a beer can under one of her feet, she
whispered, "Sorry!" Then, she climbed up the side of the bunk and
snuggled up to my roommate. For the next fifteen minutes they did

their thing. I froze, turned off my flashlight, and waited. When they were finished, she crawled back down the bunk bed and slipped out of the room as quickly as she had entered.

I can't say that event got me in the mood for my Bible study.

I was shocked when I opened my Bible to the books of Daniel and Esther and saw what my study was going to be over the next few weeks: why God took his chosen people, Israel, out of Jerusalem and into Babylon for a season of captivity.[42] As I contemplated the reasons for God's allowance of, and possible guidance into captivity, an undergirding theme emerged. God seemed to be purifying their love for him through suffering. I wondered what it meant and what it had do with me? While pondering those questions, a deep peace invaded my soul. I became immediately aware that I was in the perfect will of God, and it wasn't going to be fun. I became aware that even the deep pain I carried after Rosalyn's passing somehow was going to be used of God in my life. Though I wouldn't understand the reasons until much later, I knew that suffering would become the crucible that God would use in my life to answer my heart's cry to know Him and to identify with the world's deep needs.

Before I turned off my flashlight and lay upon my pillow for my last good night of sleep for weeks, I turned to the Psalms. David had a dramatic life, and I felt mine could be heading that direction. My eyes fell upon Psalm 126:5,6, "Those who sow in tears will reap with songs of joy. He who goes out weeping, carrying seed to sow, will return with songs of joy, carrying sheaves with him." A tear rolled down the side of my face as I contemplated the words and the unknowns of the dark season that loomed before me. That would be the last tear I would cry for a long time.

The Glories of Buthering Crab

In my family I was not known as the brother who joyfully embraced manual labor. I talked my younger brothers into doing things for me—this was easy to do during those years when they thought I had magical powers. So my first 12 hours of butchering crab was the beginning of poetic justice. I'm glad my brothers weren't there to witness it all, especially that first day.

I was the new kid on the block. All the other workers had been there for at least two summers. We stood shoulder-to-shoulder, two feet apart. Thick leather belts secured a shield, which covered our upper right hips. The live crabs were poured into a net in front of us, and we had to grab one by its legs and throw its body very quickly against the shield, while thrusting the midsection of the crab's body against a steel blade that was attached to the counter in front of us. Then the legs were removed and thrown onto a conveyor belt, all while hoping that its claws didn't find your fingers beforehand. Your mission was to butcher as many crab as possible in the shortest period of time. Five minutes into working on my technique the foreman in charge of inspecting our work yelled at me, "What are you f*in doing? Everyone is butchering twice as fast as you, so get your f*ing ass moving!" Do you think my first thought was, *God would you bless this man, and may he come to know You while I'm here?* No, my first thought was to tell him where to f*ing go!

In that moment it occurred to me that God's first goal for my season of captivity was to show me my true heart. Without my comforts and props of a strong Christian community around me, He wanted to expose the hidden darkness of my life. I had been the one who originally prayed for years, *Lord I want more of You and less of me.* Now He was taking me at my word. Spiritual pride had become a lens through which I looked at others, and when the foreman yelled at me, I wondered who he was to use such a tone with me. Didn't he know that many people loved and respected me?

Later that day, while listening to the Old Testament through my headphones, I stared at the crabs in front of me and picked up my pace until I was almost as fast as everyone else. I eased into my twelve-hour shift, listed to Garth Brooks, pop country music, and the guys bantering next to me about their latest drug heists and sex acts with whomever was available.

I had never been so excited to climb into my bunk as I was at the end of that day. Naively, I expected I would quickly fall into a deep sleep, being so tired from the many hours of work on the butcher line. No such luck. My body felt like it was still rhythmically moving with the ship. When I finally fell asleep, I'd occasionally wake up from nightmares in which the crab parents of the day's victims latched onto my body parts with their razor sharp pincers.

I whined to God for weeks. *How could You do this to me?* How could You allow the passing of my girlfriend and then bring me to this wretched place? But as I did my correspondence Bible course late at night I was continually convicted by statements like this: it took God one night to get the Israelites out of Egypt but forty years to get Egypt out of Israel. Why? Because they murmured and complained. *Did I have to be so much like them,* I thought? *Will my perpetual whining prevent me from reaching my promised land?*

After a few long weeks, I grew sick of my narcissistic droning. After all, weren't there many Christians who had suffered far more than I, and yet became better people through it? I decided that regardless of how I felt I would get up before my shift and make space for God.

One morning while I sat in a small breezeway and watched the sun rise over the purple horizon of the Bering Sea, I was struck by Paul's longing to know God in Philippians 3:10. I had memorized the words years ago and always loved the first half, but I never quite got the last bit: "I want to know Christ —yes to know the power of His resurrection," *who doesn't want that,* I thought, "and participation in His sufferings, being like Him in his death..." *What does that mean,* I wondered? That morning as the boat glided by a velvet green Aleutian island, I turned the verse into a prayer.

O Father, for years You've entrusted me with glimpses of the power of Your resurrection, through my salvation and in various countries of the world; that alone is worthy of my prayers and worship for eternity. *However, forgive me for keeping my eyes solely on my pain while being completely blind to Yours. I want to know that part of Your heart as well. How selfish of me to want just the feel-good, spectacular part of You. I want to learn how to see through the eyes of the Crucified.*

Amy Carmichael lost a husband and children for the sake of the Gospel. On the seafood processor a stanza of one of her poems gouged deep into my heart:

No wound? No scar? Yet as the Master must the servant be,
And pierced are the feet that follow Me,
But thine are whole, can he have followed far
Who has no wound, no scar? [43]

When I asked God to show me His wounds, I realized I hadn't followed His son very far. I'd always prayed pain and suffering away. I considered these thoughts after a long day of butchering crabs. While in bed I stared at the blank ceiling in front of me and realized that even after my shower I somehow still carried the scent of wet raw crab. I called out to God: *Where have You been?*

A scene from C.S. Lewis's book, *The Lion, The Witch and The Wardrobe* immediately came to mind. Aslan walked to the stone table, which was symbolic of Jesus' journey to the cross. His head was hung low as he contemplated the weight of that which he had come to give, knowing that in a moment he would encounter an unutterable aloneness. Lucy and Susan accompanied him, their hearts breaking as they leaned against his mane. Then he turned and looked at me, as if to ask, "Will you comfort me too?"

Friends share pain with friends. On the crab boat, I wondered—was it possible that Jesus wanted to share my pain and wanted me to share in His? I wondered whether Jesus has many servants but very few friends—those who will follow Him to the hard places, those who will share in His pain.

To be known by our scars we first have to be wounded. I could escape this process on the seafood processor and rebel—become bitter instead of better—or I could say with Job, "though you slay me yet will I trust in You" (Job 13:15, NKJV).

That night on my bunk I prayed, *Jesus, Aslan, You have chased me my whole life, and You have won my heart many times over. I leaned against Your mane with that poor man in England, and I will lean even now. I surrender my pursuit of comfort so I can have the ultimate privilege of being a comfort to You. Thank you for wanting to be that close to me.*

At the end of my prayer I remembered a time I leaned my head against Rosalyn's three days before she passed away. I knew she was going to die soon, and though my heart was wrecked with pain, my overriding emotion was to bring comfort to her. So one afternoon I withdrew what little money I had in my account and drove all over Newport Beach and bought things that looked like Italy: a miniature gondola, fake cypress trees, and large sunflowers. That night I got permission to paint a portion of the wall in Rosalyn's hospital room while she was asleep behind the large protective curtain that surrounded her bed. I was envisioning my artwork to resemble the backdrop of an aged Venetian wall. After four hours of painting and situating the room with my newfound treasures, I heard her begin to wake about 5:30, her usual time. That was my sign; I turned on the tape player and Pavarotti's opera music began to gently play.

"Hon, is that you?" she whispered.

I started to slowly pull the large protective curtain away, my eyes riveted upon her. Never had I seen a face become shrouded with such profound joy, comfort and sorrow as in that moment. It was too sacred to fill the air with words. I slowly, affectionately, climbed into the bed next to her and leaned my head against hers as we experienced the only Italy our eyes would ever see.

Remembering that moment on my cold bunk bed on the seafood processor that night, I felt the warmth of the presence of the One who was inviting me to lean.

Pain with God

Have you ever suffered with a friend as he or she experienced the death of a loved one? It's unforgettable. In July 14, 2004—years after my crab boat experience—I stood in a long line of people as one by one we offered our condolences to John and Bethany Murphy after the passing of their 10-month-old daughter Eliana Joy, who died of a brain tumor. I had known John for over a decade; all my memories of him were fond. I often spoke in his Snowboarders' Discipleship Training School in the Rocky Mountains of Colorado. We loved huddling around a bonfire with the students at night under a canopy of stars telling stories. Etched in my mind is the reflection of the flames dancing up and down his face as he told his wild tales, holding us spellbound one moment and breaking us opened into riotous laughter the next.

I had never seen the expression John wore on the day of his daughter's funeral. His eyes were hollow, sunken wells of lost hope. After the person in front of me offered her condolences, I stood there, frozen. Next to John stood a large picture of Eliana. She had a delightful, disarming smile, no clothes on, and red rose petals covered her body. "See my beautiful little girl," John said with the mixture of the pride of a doting father and the horror of one who had been robbed of far more than her last dance.

My eyes left the picture and fell into his. I leaned toward him and he fell into me; we caught each other and sobbed. For a moment I felt like we were one crying person.

Shared pain births a deeper intimacy than shared joy; I know this now. All the good times John and I had paled in comparison to the deep intimacy we experienced in that moment. If this is true with us, could the same be said of our God and the invitation He gives us to fellowship with His sufferings? Does He too desire this kind of oneness? Maybe suffering is the only way to get there.

Maybe there are moments God wants us to become one crying person.

Your Story

When we practice contemplation—a long loving look at the real [44] — suffering becomes both a teacher and a path of transformation. When this practice is absent, we often resort to a life of murmuring and complaining because we often desire our comfort more than we want to be Christ-like. Today let's answer the challenge of Jesus towards discomfort, explained in Luke 9:23 (ESV), "If anyone will come after me, let him deny himself, take up his cross daily, and follow me." Follow the Spirit's guide through the following spiritual exercise and discover treasures of darkness in your seasons of captivity.

1. Enter a dark room holding a lit candle. Present your life to God as you watch the flickering flame. Remember difficult seasons when you were in pain and felt alone. Pray: *Lord, search me and know me. Show me Your presence while I remember my pain. I wait on You and listen. What is Your perspective? How do You feel about this memory?*

2. In your journal write down any impressions you feel the Lord speaking to you.

Now slowly read Isaiah 53. Ask the Lord to share with you His sufferings. Express your desire to not only be His servant but also His friend.

3. While you blow the candle out pray for Christians around the world that are in pain, persecution and mental or emotional darkness. Pray that they will see God as the light in their darkness.

Notes

"The path of prayer and love,
and the path of suffering, seem
to be the two great paths of
transformation."

- *Richard Rohr, Everything Belongs*

12

My Captivity Continues

A voice echoed from the intercom, "There is no crab to butcher today, so unless otherwise notified it's a day off!" I heard those beautiful words and promptly dropped the doughnut I was holding, which tumbled into my cup of coffee, causing a splash onto the table. I paused and felt an emotion that had become foreign to me in this season of my life: joy. *A day off,* I thought, *what was that? A break from the sight, smells and vicious claws of crab for 24 glorious hours—* the bliss of not having to do a thing for a whole day exhilarated me.

Rip, who was sitting next to me, let out a snicker and said, "Did I actually see a happy face on you, Mr. Pratt? Who knew you could smile? God's given us a miracle today."

And so he had.

Later that morning I was given the choice to put in some work hours by doing what I was told would be a simple but important task. "Look at where the crab juice has been dripping all these weeks," the foreman explained as he pointed down the elevator shaft. A trail of juice had turned to ice and dropped below, beyond our sight.

"At the bottom of the elevator where we lower the pallets of crab into the freezer," he said, "there is a crab juice ice-mountain about

5 feet high. The elevator is getting stuck on top of it. With an ice pick you can remove it in a couple hours, but we want you to take 8 hours so you can be paid for a full workday. It's easy money."

"Sure," I said happily. I knew that I would be completely alone and conveniently miss a party slated for my room, one where the latest porno flick would be playing in the tiny theatre on the second floor.

For two months we had butchered crab, packed them into containers, stacked them on pallets, and sent them down the elevator into the freezer. Now I was able to spend the day on the other side of things, where the crab finished their journey before being sold in huge crates to the Japanese. I bundled up and took the metal staircase down to the freezer and stood in the bottom of the elevator shaft. I began to chip away at the crab juice ice mountain. I was blessedly alone and oddly content.

In that darkness, I began to accept this truth—suffering is a teacher, not a tormentor. This new teacher of mine was going to bring me into a greater identification with Jesus and his own suffering humanity. An emerging sense of camaraderie with Him who feels all pain set in, even though I was only pick-axing a mountain of frozen crab goo. With this fresh new perspective came the birth of a faith that was no longer built on my feelings but on truth through choice. I was choosing to believe God was good regardless of whether I felt His presence or not. Faith was becoming an inner certainty, not based on emotions, and no longer affected by negative circumstances. My love for God was becoming purified as I chipped away at the ice, not conditional upon what God gave me, or if I felt Him. He was giving me a pure love based on His worth.

While contemplating these truths, a voice cut the silence.

"Jeff are you down here?"

It was Freezer Rat, a man whose job it was to count all the pallets that came down the elevator, empty or full. Because of the crab juice ice-mountain, no pallets were allowed to come down, and he was bored.

"Jeff?" he asked again.

I wanted to be alone, so I remained silent.

"Jeff I *know* you are down here," he said harshly.

"Yes, I'm here," I said with obvious reluctance as I hit the mountain of ice even harder with the pick.

"O good I'm coming over."

A magazine filled with naked women flew through the air as he left the heap of pallets on which he had made a little bed and came to where I was working. He took an empty plastic bucket, turned it over and sat on it, facing me, right outside the elevator.

"O come on, Jeff," he pleaded, "You have 8 hours, and I have 8 hours. I'm f*in bored and I'm sure you are. You are very different from the rest of us on this boat, so I want you to start off with your earliest memory in life and bring me right up to today. Tell me your whole story. Ready... go."

I didn't want to share, and I didn't want to seize this evangelistic opportunity. But when you are a follower of Christ, the truth you've preached comes back to haunt you. I'd taught many to "die to self," and now the phrase was ringing in my inner ear. Convicted, I started with my Mormon upbringing in Endicott, New York, and walked him through my story.

At one point, he interrupted my story, and said, "We had a Mormon guy on the boat last month, and he gave me a copy of the Book of Mormon. I've been thinking of becoming an f*in Mormon." I had never heard this particular expletive used in conjunction with the word Mormon before, and it made me chuckle. After I told him what the lifestyle of a Mormon looked like he quickly changed his mind. Then I told him about my encounters with Jesus and my mission experiences.

He sat at the edge of his bucket, and occasionally shook his head and made comments like, "I thought religion was the most boring thing, but not after hearing this! When you talk about your God, it's like you are referring to someone you are deeply in love with but have not seen in long time. Like you really miss Him."

When he said those words, I realized that he had just described my captivity. I missed the One I loved. In my captivity I wanted to encounter God again and feel Him in those old familiar ways. However, I couldn't. He was doing something new, stripping away all false comforts and self-centered identities until there was nothing left but my naked will clinging to Him and Him alone. He knew my appetite for Him grew best in the dark.

A Near Fatal Accident

Hours later, I finished telling my story to the Freezer Rat, and he asked, "You were once an aspiring journalist, and you had a nice girlfriend and a promising future. Now you have nothing and are stuck on this hell of a boat. If you were to die today, would you have done anything different?"

I thought for a moment before answering and then said in confidence, "There are some things I would have done differently, but even though it's a difficult season in my life I can honestly say that if I were to die today, there has been nothing like following and knowing Jesus. I wouldn't trade this kind of life with Him for all the wealth in the world."

As I said those words, six pallets were pushed into the elevator shaft five stories above me. They came barreling down, and one hit me on top of my head, knocking me unconscious. My body collapsed onto the half-chipped crab juice ice mountain. Scrambling, the Freezer Rat pulled my body out from under the pallet and laid my head on his lap. My eyes were rolled back and blood was dripping out of my mouth. An emergency crew came with a stretcher. They'd later tell me that they thought my neck was broken, and that I might die at any given moment. As they bent down to lift my body onto the stretcher, to their shock, I quickly leaned forward and robotically stood to my feet. After I zipped up my jacket, I turned away from the crew and began to walk away. Stunned, they followed me.

I walked out of the freezer while I held a washcloth on the right side of my head where I was bleeding. I didn't move my left shoulder or let my arm sway because it was swollen and in pain.

In the meantime the crew had heard about the accident, but there was a bit of confusion on the fifth floor as to where the pallets had originated. Every pallet, empty or full, had to be accounted for. Five pallets were missing from the sixth floor, and only one had hit me, so some of the crew began to look for the remaining pallets. My roommate Rip was among them. In his search, he leaned over and looked down the elevator shaft. What he saw made the hair on his arms stand on end. He whistled for the crew, and there, suspended in air in the elevator shaft as if they were floating, were the remaining five missing pallets. As Rip stretched out his arm to touch them, they immediately fell down the shaft and landed where I had been standing just moments before.

Rip turned to the crew and said, "I knew our roommate was strange... Jeff's God is God."

For the next hour, as word of the miracle spread throughout the boat, you could hear port hole windows opening, and pornography and other paraphernalia being crammed through them to forever sink to the bottom of the sea as a holy God walked that boat.

While I sat in my room with some of the medical personnel, a lady handed me an envelope from a friend in New Zealand. It only contained a Bible verse typed on a small piece of paper that read: "When the enemy comes in like a flood, the Spirit of the Lord will lift up a standard against him" (Isaiah 59:19, NKJV).

An Emergency Room Offer

Because of the incident, the medical crew required me to undergo a CT Scan. The closest emergency room with the needed device was in Anchorage, and that afternoon a boat took me to Dutch Harbor where I caught a flight. After the CT Scan, the doctor brought me the results.

"I'm not a person who believes in miracles," he said. "Taking into account the distance the pallet fell, and its weight, you should not be alive, but aside from a minor concussion, there's nothing wrong with you. The swelling in your shoulder has already gone down. It's amazing." He reached for a stack of papers and handed them to me. "On top of it all, I have other good news. If you sign these papers the company will be sued because the accident was their fault. You may be feeling fine now, but you never know, Jeff. Ten years from now you may get headaches from this, or sudden dizziness. Who knows? By suing them they'll have to fly you home to Seattle tomorrow and in six months you'll have a whole lot of money."

Wow, I thought, *God saves my life one day, and gives me a large payday the next; it doesn't get much better than this!* But another voice whispered, "Jeff, your season of captivity isn't over yet, go back to the ship."

I considered the voice I'd learned to call the Spirit of God.

"No thanks," I told the doctor, "I need to return to the boat."

"I think you were hit harder than I thought," he said.

That night I recorded this in my journal: *Never flee from your season of captivity. You think it's hard now; if you escape you'll have to go around the same mountain again, and it may be even harder next time.*

So, twenty-four hours after my accident, I walked back up the gangway of the boat docked in Dutch Harbor. I caught a glimpse of the top of Rip's head as I stepped aboard, and I could see that he was mopping the deck. When he saw my face, he dropped the mop and stared at me as if he were seeing a ghost. No one on the boat thought they'd see me again. They figured I'd do what almost anyone would do: sue the company and happily fly home a richer man.

"What are you doing back here?" Rip asked, obviously perplexed.
"Well, it's hard to explain," I said, trying to think of an explanation.
"Just give me one good reason," he persisted.
"Ok," I said, pausing with my luggage as I looked into his eyes.
"You and I never became friends the first time around," I replied.
It was the first time I saw Rip speechless for a moment.

"Me?" he said in unbelief, "How could someone good like you ever want to be friends with a bastard like me?" Now I was speechless, but only for a second.

"I'm not entirely sure," I replied.

Quietly he helped me take my luggage to my new room.

A Gracious Hope

Salmon season began the day after I returned to the boat.

I was walking down a staircase when a Hispanic man brushed by me. I felt something within me suddenly move. I said, "Excuse me sir, do you know Jesus?" In broken English he replied, "Yes, I know Jesus; I met him on a great white ship in Lazaro Cardnes, Mexico!" What are the chances, I thought? This man came to know God through the ministry of the *Anastasis* while I was onboard during my Mercy Ships stint.

Together, we walked to the deck to receive our assignments. And of all the 120-crew members aboard the boat, my new friend Ernesto worked directly across from me.

We worked together and spoke about Jesus. Ernesto's presence showed me how God often offers hope, not relief, in suffering; I wasn't being rescued from my captivity yet, but I was given grace to persevere.

Day after day, I showed up to rack salmon and to lead my crew, inwardly complaining. I was in survival mode. But there was Ernesto, working across from me and joyfully singing songs of praise. Sometimes, it made me angry. Often I expressed my frustration.

One day he saw my scowl, threw a fish down onto the conveyor belt, and with great frustration said, "Jeff, since the miracle, all the eyes of the crew are on you. But Jeff, you aren't happy... get happy!" I wanted to tell him where to go, but he was right. I was just surviving my captivity, not embracing it. The words of Ecclesiastes 9:10 found me out, "Whatever your hands find to do, do it with all of your might," as unto Jesus. So, that afternoon I asked the foreman on our deck, "Sir, every time you walk by and inspect our work, a bunch of guts and fins slide by us on the conveyor belt. Once you walk by us, and turn your back, will you allow us to hit you with a clump of the guts and fins below your neck? If you can't guess which ones of us did it, could we get a point?"

Confused he just glared at me for a moment, and then said, "Jeff, you are f*ing stranger than I thought. Why would you want to do that?"

"Sir, the rackers are very bored. The machinery is too loud for us to talk to one another. The game might help us have some fun, and it will make time go by faster. Please let us play; I promise we will not break up our working pace." To my shock he was deeply moved, and said, "You want to do this for your men?"

"Yes," I replied. "They are my friends."

More than the miracle of the floating pallets, it was this game that warmed the hearts of the crew towards the Gospel. Perhaps embracing my humanity allowed the crew to accept God's divinity; they saw that I was like them, and this led them to want to be more like me, a joy-filled follower of Jesus.

While playing the game, within a week we became the fastest salmon rackers in the fleet.

Homeward Bound

"Everyone to the bow of the ship for an important announcement," came the stern voice of the captain over the intercom. Surprised by the abruptness of his words and the tone of his voice, we all sullenly pushed our salmon racks aside and gathered on the deck. A rare hush fell over the crowd as we stood quietly under the intense warmth of the noonday sun.

Once the captain arrived, he stepped up onto one of the forklifts so that we could all see him. Without a greeting or any usual trivial comments he said, "The hard news is this: as of this moment salmon season is now over. All of your contracts are cut, except those who work in the galley and engine room."

An immediate groan of shock and disappointment permeated the crowd.

He continued, "Another piece of bad news: we are the farthest ship out on the Bering Sea. All the other seafood processors are going to fill the ports of Alaska, so there will be no berths available to us. We can't drop you off in a port in British Columbia because we sail under an American flag. There is only one open berth on the west coast. We sail tomorrow for Seattle, Washington."

God is bringing me home, I inwardly gasped. *He is ending my captivity, in His time and in His way.* I was stunned and had to let the words sink in before I actually surrendered to their reality; the place of my captivity would become the place that would carry me home.

Though most of the crew was disappointed over the loss of their jobs, you couldn't tell by how they partied as we sailed alongside Vancouver Island and into the San Juan's. When I saw the 14,409-foot peak of Mount Rainer cloaked in snow, sitting like a majestic guardian over the glittering towers of Seattle, I knew my promised land was soon coming. *Once they lower the gangway*, I thought, *I'm going to run down it and kiss the ground!*

I rushed to my room to get my luggage, when to my shock there was Rip, sitting on my makeshift couch, shaved for the first time. "Wow, you almost look handsome," I said. He didn't chuckle or even look at me, he just stared soberly down at the ground. I never saw him this serious, and at first I didn't know what to say.

"What's the matter Rip?" I asked. "You haven't lost your job. You will still work in the engine room. How come you look so sad?"

He didn't respond for a moment, but then slowly turned and looked at me.

"Every day that I've been here," he said, "when I've seen you, I've seen a God of love looking at me. Today you leave, and I won't see Him anymore."

He paused as if he was trying to control his emotions and voice inflections.

"I was wondering," he said as tears filled his eyes, "if a God like yours would ever want a loser like me? I've done so many evil things in my life, if you only knew."

He dropped his head in sorrow.

I slowly knelt beside him, stunned by the softness of his heart and his repentant plea. "God has been waiting for you since the day you were born," I said, "waiting to have you as His son."

Rip got down on his knees, made the sign of the cross, and with a furrowed brow asked me, "I haven't prayed in so long. What do I say?"

"Just tell God how you feel," I assured him.

As I watched my friend Rip talk to God, surrendering his life to Him, I had an epiphany: one soul brought into the Kingdom of God is worth more than all the pain of captivity. In that moment God showed me the value of a soul.

Sadly, I never saw or heard from Rip again. But over a decade later I was speaking at The Lord's Land YWAM base in Mendocino, California, and had finished sharing the Alaska captivity story. One of the students mentioned during the break, "How crazy, I have heard that story before, but from a different vantage point—through the eyes of the man looking down the elevator shaft at the floating pallets. You call him Rip."

"Where did you see him?" I asked, in utter shock.

"He works at Teen Challenge in San Francisco. I heard him share his testimony with a group of men who were in rehab. My brother was in rehab. The man said, 'There was a man on my last seafood processor that told me there is a love that is better than life. There is a love that will not let you go. I chose to believe him, and you can believe him too.'"

Your Story

In our seasons of captivity there is a mission to be found: It is God's formational work in us, and His mission through us—so that in our pain we can learn to love. We are in desperate need of mercy to accomplish this, especially when difficult seasons seem to last longer than we ever anticipated, so we turn to the Jesus prayer, used throughout the centuries, for guidance and grace.

1. The Jesus Prayer, "*Lord Jesus Christ, son of God, have mercy on me a sinner,*" is often repeated continually as part of an ascetic practice particularly esteemed by the desert fathers. It's a method of bringing about *the prayer of the heart*, which is what Paul refers to in 1 Thessalonians 5:17 as "unceasing prayer." I repeated the Jesus Prayer in a difficult season of life, and on one occasion awoke in the middle of the night and could hear my spirit praying the plea to God. This was followed by an overwhelming sense of peace.

Reflect upon a difficult season in your life that is unresolved in your heart. Slowly begin to say the Jesus Prayer repeatedly. Freely receive what God wants to give you, be it forgiveness, healing, grace to persevere, or wisdom. Practice this before you go to bed and when you get up in the morning for three consecutive days.

2. Read Luke 15:3-5 and ask God to show you the worth of a soul. As an aspiring contemplative activist share *the love that is better than life* (Psalm 63:3) with someone at least once a week over the course of the next three months, journal your experiences.

Notes

"Define yourself radically loved as one beloved of God. God's love for you and His choice of you constitute your worth."

- Brennan Manning, *Abba's Child*

13

Eternal Realities

My season of captivity on the seafood processor in Alaska was an experience that purified my awareness of what really matters in life—the eternal. Suffering has a way of doing that. While boarding the Mukilteo Ferry to Whidbey Island to return to my parents' home, I noticed the dark green and blue hues of the Puget Sound, which seemed richer and deeper than I remembered. The lingering embraces of my mom and dad upon my arrival felt less like an appropriate parental gesture and more like genuine affection from the ache of missing. I realized that nothing had really changed but me. I saw things differently, experienced life in a new, more full way. The temporary and the trivial were where they belonged, in the background, while I enjoyed the nostalgic cry of the seagull and inhaled the banter of friends. Effortlessly, I was finding life in every breath as a humbled fugitive released from my prison of self. I remember thinking, *How can I live in this acute awareness of treasured, eternal realities? Must I continually be thrown into the crucible of suffering to look at life through the eyes of the Crucified?*

Yes, endurance had trained me through suffering to begin to see the world and myself more clearly. Now a season of another kind of training was about to emerge: training in true contemplative vision, not of myself but of God.

Faithful Family Rhythms and Another Move

My parents' house on Whidbey Island seemed to never change. My siblings were still at home—except for Steve and Tim. Young people were always crashing the house—whether for long term or for shorter stints—no matter how many years passed. This had been a minor frustration when I wanted a respite between major mission trips, but now I found it to be beautiful.

The morning hours were still in the house as my siblings and Mom spent time with God. The house was quiet until10:30, the time that my siblings started their home school studies. That's usually where quiet ended. Evenings smelled of spaghetti, or pizza, and the riotous activity of youth coming and going filled every room. It was a season of activity and rest, family and friends. It was a sweet time.

After being at home for a month, I received a call from Jack Minton, a friend with whom I had worked on the *Anastasis*. He told me that Last Days Ministries, led by Melody Green, had recently joined YWAM, and they needed help changing their Intensive Christian Training Program into an YWAM Discipleship school through adding the component of a mission outreach. "You have done a great job of leading mission outreaches," Jack said, "and they could really use your help." Upon hearing the offer I immediately thought of the Keith Green Memorial concert I attended years ago, where I made my public declaration of my mission call. Still burning within me was his life message—*no compromise*—a call to a radical devotion to God and his mission for the world. Since returning from the Alaskan fishing boat, I was yearning to invest myself into discipleship and mission and live wholeheartedly for eternity. So, after a few days of prayerful consideration and consulting close friends and my parents, all seemed to confirm this was a positive direction for my life. Right before my thirtieth birthday I moved onto the red dusty dirt roads of Last Days Ministries in east Texas.

I spent six years with LDM and Mercy Ships in Texas, and over those years I learned about how Jesus spent His hours and His days. I studied the ways in which He spent His time, how He spent His days in prayer and serving the sick and the poor. I, on the other hand, spent little time doing those things. I concluded I wasn't a very good Christ-follower. I loved Jesus in word but not in deeds. I adopted Christian language and even lived out some of the ideals, but my habits and disciplines didn't always follow. I set out to change this.

Thankfully, I was blessed with a wonderful team of friends and co-workers at LDM and Mercy Ships, friends who wanted to explore the radical discipleship of monasticism—following Jesus as a way of life. We wanted to form a Christian community of gospel practitioners, those who elevate the doing of the gospel over just talking about it. And as we considered how to better practice the gospel, we heard from various speakers and teachers, disciples who mentored us in the ways of Jesus. We read book after book hoping to understand how to live a more authentic Christian life. At the time I was reading a book by Brennan Manning, *Abba's Child*. A phrase in his book touched a deep need in my life, "...the heart of it all is this: to make the Lord and His immense love for you constitutive of your personal worth. Define yourself radically loved as one beloved by God. God's love for you and His choice of you constitute your worth. Accept that, and let it become the most important thing in your life." [45] The book by Manning struck a nerve, and I invited him to come speak to us.

The time with Manning was wonderful, and during one discussion I confessed some of my struggles. I was frustrated by my oversensitivity to the criticism of others, I told him. Though I had grown past caring what the general public thought of me, the assessment of my peers was all too important to me. How did I know this? In telling stories I would slightly exaggerate, make the narrative a little funnier, or emotionally more moving than the actual reality. I asked him how I could be anchored in my given, unearned identity as one beloved by God and break this cycle in my life?

His piercing blue eyes met mine, and he said in his deep voice, "Radical solitude." He proceeded to explain that central to the life of Jesus was the practice of silence, solitude and prayer and that if we are true Christ-followers, we will walk in these steps. Upon hearing this, one of our zealous staff members took the rest of the day off to head up into the oak-wooded plains of the back property to be alone with God.

The next day the zealous staffer approached Brennan rather deflated and said, "I did what you said. I spent all afternoon and evening with God in silence, solitude, and prayer and didn't really get anything. I wonder if I was doing it wrong."

Brennan showed no expression. He just proceeded to say, "Every Friday night I used to visit a friend, and we would get caught up, usually over a piece of cheesecake. But during one season of our friendship, my friend stopped serving cheesecake due to tight finances, and I stopped showing up as much. Then eventually I stopped visiting all together. A couple of weeks later I received a call from him that was rather embarrassing. 'Brennan,' he said, 'did you stop coming to visit me on Friday nights because I stopped serving cheesecake?' I blushed."

"In cultivating an awareness of the present risenness of Jesus through the disciplines," Brennan said, "you measure success by simply showing up and shutting up! God is worthy of our time and attention, regardless of whether we receive any emotional payback, or profound revelations, or spiritual cheesecake. He's just happy you showed up."

I considered Manning's words and began to practice silence and solitude. And months later, in that practice, I stumbled upon Paul's words in Colossians 1: 25–27. The passage reads, "...the commission God gave me to present to you the word of God in its fullness—*the mystery* that has been hidden for ages and generations, but is now disclosed to the Lord's people. To them God has chosen to make known among the Gentiles the glorious riches of this *mystery*, which is *Christ in you, the hope of glory.*" (Emphasis added.) This is when it dawned on me—*who doesn't want the word of God in its fullness, that mystery that has been hidden for generations?* I determined in that moment I would do whatever it took to unravel this mystery of all mysteries, the greatest eternal reality—no matter the cost.

Divine Union Finds Me

I sailed into Catalina Island, twenty miles off the coast of Los Angeles. The town of Avalon sprawled out before me. It is nestled amongst steep hills, stacked with porched homes reminiscent of Italy's Amalfi Coast, but miniature in size. I knew Catalina well; its small number of permanent residents, its protected conservancy, home to wild buffalo and other wildlife. This was the backdrop for my initial experiment with the spiritual practices of solitude and prayer, my attempt to unpack the mystery. I guess I figured that if the training didn't go so well, at least I'd have fly fishing tours, diving, and snorkeling right at my fingertips.

I'll never forget my first couple of days. My goal was to begin to experience Paul's mystery of all mysteries. I found a beautiful spot on top of a ridge that overlooked a small turquoise bay to my left and all Avalon Bay to my right. As I sat on a wall under a lone tree, I felt like I was leaning against the edge of a tropical resort postcard. Next to me was my Bible, journal, and Henry Nouwen's tiny book *The Way of the Heart. Ok*, I thought, *I'm ready to encounter God in silence and solitude and to experience His love.*

After reading Psalm 139, I prayed, worshipped and listened. I envisioned Jesus looking at me smiling and pictured myself leaning into His embrace, as a respectful son would joyfully surrender to the affection of his father. I attempted to slow down my racing thoughts. Then I immediately had an awakening—to the succulent smells of BBQ

Buffalo burgers and waffle cones from the stores beneath me.
Maybe I need to meditate on some literature from a great mystic,
I thought. *Perhaps it would help me focus.* I noticed earlier there was
a poem by St. John of The Cross; called "Living Flame of Love," in
another book I had with me. I began to read it, phrase by phrase, but
it felt too humanly romantic in its depiction of God's love for us. I
turned my head to the left, away from Avalon, from what I thought
represented the world and its appetites. I looked down onto the bay
off Descanso Beach. My eyes latched onto two guys being pulled on
a mammoth inner tube behind a speedboat, shouting playful words at
the driver, taunting him to knock them off. *How fun,* I thought,
remembering the times when, off the coast of northern California, my
brothers and I would all balance on a log in the ocean and see who
could stay on it the longest. I was still distracted.

This feels like a waste of time, I thought. Then I realized, I wasn't
showing up and shutting up. I decided to stop fighting the distractions,
to let them come and go without getting frustrated.

Once I allowed my mind to do its own thing for a while, everything
came into focus. I began to repeat slowly, "Christ in you the hope of
glory," then I cut one of the last words off from the verse, and slowly
said it again, personalizing the text, *"Christ in me the hope,"* then
"Christ in me." There was just one word left. I whispered *"Christ."*
I waited, and after a while, to my surprise, I was enveloped by a
remarkable sense of peace. I lingered there for a while, and then
retreated back to the town.

The next day, I revisited the same place. I showed up and practiced
silence. Centering seemed easier. And as I listened, as I rested, I was
moved to make a promise to God. I would do whatever it took to taste
the fullness of the Gospel—to discover for myself the Mystery.

My third day was a significant day, a day of resurrection. After an
hour of worshipping and reading scriptures during a moment of stillness, an image popped into my mind. I remembered my mother in the
last days of one of her pregnancies. I remembered her loving, nurtur-

ing, protecting ways. She was a gentle mother, and she recognized the life inside her and stewarded her pregnancy well.

Why hadn't I considered mom's pregnancies and the warm memories of her tending to new life inside her? As I contemplated this, I stumbled upon Zephaniah 3:17, "The Lord your God is with you, the Mighty Warrior who saves. He will take great delight in you; in His love He will no longer rebuke you, but will rejoice over you with singing." *Rejoice over me*, I thought, *with my inferiorities and insecurities?* Then in the depth of my own contemplation, I felt the movement of Life in me—a powerful sacred force. An eruption of ecstatic delight washed over me, not sweet or sentimental, but tidal in its magnitude. *He is in me, loving me, right here, right now*, I thought, and I became suddenly aware that I was part of a larger Life being lived, a broader prayer being prayed, a greater Love being loved. I was awakened to Mystery inside me and I was undone. I sat there frozen in a timeless space.

I sat in the moment, and then glanced at the poem from St. John of the Cross, the one too layered with emotion just two days before. Now it perfectly described what happened to me:

"O Living Flame of Love,
How gently and lovingly
Thou wakest in my bosom,
Where alone Thou secretly dwellest;
And in Thy sweet breathing
Full of grace and glory
How tenderly Thou fillest me with Thine love." [46]

At the end of that day I was immediately struck by my primary purpose in life and the true meaning of *holiness:* to nurture, protect and welcome this Life that was within me and to carry Jesus as Mary did—with a reverent fiery wonder. Now I knew my life was not my own.

I left my panoramic precipice and headed down the road back to Avalon, my renewed spiritual vision catching all the nuances of color around me. A little grin crossed my face as I pondered the infinite reality— God is closer to me than the Catalina air. He was in me, this mystery. Why hadn't I noticed this before?

Your Story

Central to the lives of contemplative activists throughout the centuries is the reality of our union with Christ and the blessedness of creation. Here I'll lead you through two practices that will purify your awareness of the mystery of all mysteries—Christ in us the hope of glory—while you allow creation to help lead you there.

1. Romans 1:20 says, "For since the creation of the world God's invisible qualities—His eternal power and divine nature—have been clearly seen from what has been made..." Walk, or drive to a place that you find beautiful. As you reflect on your surroundings, listen, smell and breathe slowly, then write down, or draw/paint, what invisible qualities of God you sense around you. Consider how creation is not just nature. It's sacramental, in that it is infused with the presence and glory of God— and so are you!

After you practice contemplative prayer, recite Romans 8:11 (*The Message*) aloud—"God lives and breathes in me as He did in Jesus." Personalize the text: "You live and breathe in me as you did in Jesus." Repeat this phrase several times a day until you begin to believe it.

2. Find a place where you can only hear the sounds of creation, and practice silence, solitude, and prayer for two hours. (Remember *success is showing up and shutting up.*) Ask God, "What do You feel about me?" Listen and journal any impression you receive from Him as you slowly meditate on the following verses:

I determined the exact time of your birth and where you would live.
Acts 17:26

I brought you forth on the day you were born.
Psalm 71:6

I am not distant and angry, but am the complete expression of love.
1 John 4:16

It is my desire to lavish my love on you.
1 John 3:1

Simply because you are my child and I am your father.
I John 3:1

Every good gift that you receive comes from my hand.
James 1:17

For I am a provider and I meet all your needs.
Matthew 6:31-33

My plan for your future has always been filled with hope.
Jeremiah 29:11

Because I love you with an everlasting love.
Jeremiah 31:3

And I rejoice over you with singing.
Zephaniah 3:17

For you are my treasured possession.
Exodus 19:5

I desire to establish you with all my heart and all my soul.
Jeremiah 32:41

And I want to show you great and marvelous things.
Jeremiah 33:3

If you seek me with all of your heart, you will find Me.
Deuteronomy 4:29

Delight in me and I will give you the desires of your heart.
Psalm 37:4

For it is I who gave you those desires.
Philippians 2:13

As a shepherd carries a lamb, I have carried you close to my heart.
Isaiah 40:11

*For a more exhaustive selection of verses go to The Father's love letter website (www.fathersloveletter.com), from where the above verses were taken.

Notes

"If we have no peace it is
because we have forgotten
that we belong to each other."

- Mother Teresa

14

The Beloved Community

Mark was only a few feet behind me as we ascended one of the lower Himalayan peaks with a group of friends. Suddenly, the rocks beneath one of his feet gave way. I immediately reached out to grab him by the hand but to my shock he quickly recoiled, which sent him sliding down a long sheet of gravel rocks. The incident could easily have been prevented if he had simply taken my hand.

Mark was an extreme introvert with a cold and distant temperament. He was in Nepal for ten days to explore the Himalayas and to visit a friend who was on my team. He had joined us for a hike which meant to serve as a diversion from an intense time of ministry in a nearby village.

Later that night I would learn some of the details of his story.

When Mark was twelve years old, he was climbing a tree in the front yard of his home when he became stuck. After he realized how high he had climbed he panicked and froze in fear, gripping the branch that was next to him. He yelled, "Dad help me, I can't get down!"

His father, who was reading on the porch, heard the terror in his son's voice and immediately began to climb the tree. Once he was a few yards from his son and saw him shaking, he said, "Son, it's going be okay, just let me help you." His father leaned towards Mark and attempted to grab him with one of his arms when Mark, in fear, abruptly pushed him away. This caused his father to lose his balance and step back onto a branch that was too weak to hold his weight, making it immediately crumble, sending him falling backwards into the branches below.

Since the day of that accident Mark's father has been confined to a wheel chair.

The evening after I had tried to help Mark on the mountainside, and before I heard his story, the group of us gathered around a camp-fire to talk about the day. Mark had isolated himself and was sitting on a log in the shadows of the trees. I walked over to him to try and draw him into the group. "Come and join us," I said, but he just stared ahead. I felt a strong impression from the Spirit within me—God wanted me to participate with Him in touching the life of this young man. I reached out my hand to him and said, "Mark it's going to be okay, let me help you." In the process of him pushing me away I said, "God finds you worth loving Mark."

He immediately began to cry, tears that led to deep sobs, as he buried his face in his hands and moaned, "I'm so sorry Dad. Look what I've done to you. I'm not worthy of anyone's help, how could anyone love me?"

Once Marks's emotions subsided we talked, prayed, and he shared with me some of his life story. Later we joined the group around the campfire. The next few days he decided to stay with us and help serve the village people. He seemed like a different person—fully emotion-ally engaged and wielding a great sense of humor. It was as if another person had emerged, a person easy to love.

Telling Our Stories

Before I adopted Brandon and Patrick I began teaching a series entitled, "The Father Heart of God." I taught it in various parts of the world and gained great fulfillment in the activism of "binding up the brokenhearted" and being a temporary "father to the fatherless." Part of the teaching experience involved participants sharing their stories.

I continue to teach about God's father heart, and in recent years on our Axiom Pilgrimages and retreats I've been struck by the healing power that comes while exposing our lives to each other, and ultimately, to the Father. The healing has not only come in our emotions but also our minds. Neurologist Curt Thompson, M.D. says, "When a person tells her story and is truly heard and understood, both she and the listener undergo actual changes in their brain circuitry. They feel a great emotional and relational connection, decreased anxiety, and greater awareness of and compassion for others' suffering." [47] This exploration would later lead me to study what it means to have the mind of Christ and the integrated, contemplative mind. However, long before I ventured in that direction, when I saw Mark transformed in Nepal through sharing his story, I knew I was moving into a different season of ministry. It would no longer be "just God and me" but about the community of faith.

There comes a time in our lives when our story alone with God no longer defines us; when the "God and me" becomes "God and we" as our stories become intertwined with the narratives of other like-minded people who yearn to be God's real presence in the world. And what started in Texas as a personal relationship became a communal one, as twenty-five of us joined together to embark on a God-inspired journey with a greater understanding of what Dietrich Bonhoeffer and Dr. Martin Luther King called, "The Beloved Community."

The "Beloved Community," Rev. Janet Robertson Duggin notes is a "people who believe deeply that they are loved by God and that everyone around them is loved by God too; people who believe this deeply enough that it shapes who they are and how they live their lives and how they will deal with their own and each other's broken-ness." [48] We wanted to be this kind of people.

My three years with the Last Days Ministries Community was a powerful season of training in understanding the eternal realities of community life, particularly in relation to my own brokenness. While I made time every day to respond to the personal homeward call of John 15:4 (The Message), "Live in me. Make your home in me as I do in you," and to discover the mystery of Christ in me, I realized that in the same scripture passage was another eternal reality equally as breathtaking. John 15:12 reads, "My command is this: love each other as I have loved you. Greater love has no man than this that he lay down his life for his *friends.*"

A Trailer-Land of Friendship

The original pioneers of what would become YWAM Axiom, and eventually Axiom Monastic Community, met on the dusty red dirt roads of a trailer park in east Texas; a place that housed most of the staff of Last Days Ministries. When he was alive, Keith Green was determined for the ministry to live simply. He didn't want to spend money beautifying staff accommodations or paving the roads; he'd rather have those funds go towards eternal purposes. I appreciated his values and actually loved the simple campground feel of what we fondly called *Trailer-Land.* However, living in East Texas in trailers also made it easy for the tarantulas, brown recluse spiders, water moccasins, and June bugs to make their home with us. If that wasn't exciting enough, the Last Days Ministries property was built in Smith County, where the weather storms and tornadoes weren't always predictable. Trailer dwellers as we were, these physical realities were the catalysts that kept our faith alive!

When you live in simplicity, it is easier to put your time and attention into what's most valuable in life, the eternal realities we've been exploring. With simple lives, removed from the clutter of things, we're able to have time and space to not only come home to God but to come home to one another. That quirky place we referred to as "Trailer-Land" became the backdrop for a small group to learn that we belonged to each other, to our hopes, dreams and eventual brokenness. We didn't know at the time that years later, after we moved to New England and created Axiom, most of our lives would become less simple as we took on either itinerate ministries, larger families, or various forms of global activism. So I look back at our time in East Texas as our *Wonder Years*, reminiscent of the popular TV series in the 1990s. We were like adult children, fully engaged with our discipleship programs and leadership of the ministry, but with plenty of time to laugh and play together; I think that's what kept us healthy.

Rob Morris was my first friend who was also a co-worker. He and his wife Christel had two kids, Amber and Tyler, and were from upstate New York. I chuckle now, when I think of how they would have reacted then if they had known they would be adopting five kids in the years to come. Their trailer was across from the runway where Keith Green's plane crashed in 1983. In the evening, their trailer served as an idyllic hangout, a place to have a bonfire and "talk story." We made the most of those days, those common spaces. One rainy evening we invited a couple of our staff friends over to watch the movie *Arachnophobia*. The memorable moment of the night was during the scene where one of the thousands of spiders comes flying through a tube and into the face of a woman. Rob and I had the room nice and dark, so at that moment we sent a plastic spider gliding through the air on fishing line toward the ladies on the couch, causing them to scream and jump over the coffee table!

Playing together was a room in what I would later call The Beloved Community House that we frequented often as a group of friends and co-workers; it gave us courage to enter the often challenging rooms of commitment and confession. Yet we learned that as we made space to enjoy each other and to be alone with God together, vulnerability in worship and prayer and unity in our vision casting seemed to flow naturally. These priorities became nonnegotiable to us, and within the course of leading one training school our times together began to feel like family.

A Spirituality of Imperfection

If you were to see me back in the mid-90s in Trailer-Land you would say I looked quite out of place. In my physical appearance, perfection was my goal; my hair was always perfect and rather immovable. I sported a Magnum P.I. mustache and usually wore a tie—cool ties were the trend—so my collection ranged from sheik impressionistic designs to my favorite Statue of Liberty King Kong print. However, contrary to how I appeared I had begun to make a shift in the kind of Christianity I was living, from a spirituality of perfection where there was just "God and me," to a *spirituality of imperfection* where there was "God plus others and me." [49]

One catalyst to this change was an observation I made of Brennan Manning when he came to teach at our ministry. In the afternoons he would often attend AA groups. He wasn't afraid of showing weakness or acknowledging his need for others' support. I was. I still struggled with sexualizing my need for intimacy in my mind, especially when I lacked close friendships. As I made steps towards risking vulnerability and sharing my imperfections with those I was leading at LDM, the very love I needed began to heal my heart.

In my younger years I had viewed the Christian life as a solo journey up a staircase, and I was ascending from one truth to another. The hope was to reach a certain depth of maturity and then spend the rest my life leading others there—to my relatively perfect, yet isolated place. However, I began to see that a *spirituality of imperfection* seemed to be more true to life. In spiritual imperfection, I unlearned more than I learned, and became stronger in understanding my weakness. It was in my lack of trying to appear that I'd *arrived*, that true eternal friendships were forged and I learned to have genuine compassion on others.

I learned that the goal in our spiritual lives is not to grasp another truth so we may ascend to the next step on the staircase of an ego-driven race to perfection, but the goal is to descend into the depths of our true self—with trusted friends—and find a perfect loving God there. Johnny Sertin, who stood with me in front of the crumbling Berlin Wall in 1988, shocked me into this realization by saying to me when he came to teach at LDM, "Jeff, I don't want the processed version of you. I want the raw real you before you've prayed through your issues and patched yourself up—that person is far easier to love and has much more compassion on me."

At Last Day Ministries my spiritual perspective began to change from being centered on my own personal growth to a life that was focused on seeking and finding God together as a community; one is narcissistic, and the other is true Christianity.

The lyrics to Leonard Cohen's song "Anthem" catches the heart behind this type of spirituality. The troubadour sings, "Ring the bell that still can ring, forget your perfect offering, there is a crack in everything, that's how the light gets in." When I arrived in Texas I had journeyed long enough with God to see the futility of living in denial of my cracks, but I still tried to hide them from others and to present to the world the idealized version of myself. This isolated me from the very intimacy I needed from others and kept the liberating light of God from touching my fractures. Within a beloved community I was to discover that our cracks are not only to be acknowledged but also *celebrated*, for they are bearers of light, healing, and identification with the world.

My Parent's Spiritual Journey

My parents couldn't have been more excited that I was part of a ministry that had strongly impacted their lives. They felt that Keith Green's message and music, which challenged people to a sold-out radical life of *no compromise* for God, was the closest form of authentic Christianity that existed. This was what they felt Jesus meant when he said, "Come follow me." Also, after leaving Mormonism it was difficult for Mom and Dad to find a church that they felt held to this standard and operated as a beloved community, not just a "teaching center." (This was a term that several of my British friends have used to refer to our American church construct).

Mom's prophetic nature was prone to be judgmental, thus no church seemed Christ-centered enough. And yet she was hardest on herself. Even with the consistency of her daily times with God, she often didn't feel she was spiritual enough or worthy of the love of God.

Mom had a respect for my relationship with God and experience in missions, so she would often ask me for spiritual guidance. I remember several walks with her along the beaches of Whidbey Island, Washington, where she told me, with tears in her eyes, "Sometimes I have wondered if I'm even saved."

What compounded Mom's sense of guilt was that in the 90's she began to experience mild forms of dementia. This often prevented her from experiencing joy in life and made it difficult for her to relax. This was accentuated at holidays, which used to be her favorite times with the family. Mom could no longer enjoy the commotion of our fun activities and to our extreme regret she didn't enjoy cooking anymore! An end of an era had sadly arrived. Now our goal was to keep Mom from getting stressed-out.

My parents came alive when they visited me in communities like Last Days Ministries. Eventually they began to make retirement plans to buy their first home in east Texas so that they could be part of our beautiful community.

The Community and The Call

The common bond that held us together as a team of friends at Last Days Ministries is best described through a statement I wrote for a school we would lead a couple of years later at the Mercy Ship training center just a few miles away. I wrote, "Amidst the riotous clamor of this present age, can anyone hear through the maddening crowd, *it's time to get back to Jesus alone?*" We all felt a radical pull to the centrality of Christ in our community, to becoming his true followers. We were exploring what it meant to be an authentic community, and everyone on the team had some contribution towards this call in both character and gifting.

Whenever Mike Ash stood in front of our community and led us in worship, in a matter of minutes you'd forget he was there as your heart became transfixed on the beauty and wonder of Jesus. Mike's gentle presence alongside his beautiful wife Christine's humble self-deprecating nature made them invaluable.

Rick and Brenda Lewis, with their children Jordan and Ricci, were also musicians. Their home was the fun place to hang out with food and much laughter, and they greeted everyone who entered their door. Rick was the kind of person for whom *what you see is what you get*. He never carried any spiritual pretense, and he always had a joke or story that would make you laugh, even if you felt like you shouldn't be laughing. As an extreme extrovert, Brenda's personality captured the meaning of the word *community*; she made everyone feel immediately valued and was never happy unless she felt each person was having a good time.

My friend Rob was an extrovert, too. His deep commanding voice and charismatic personality made his short muscular stature seem much larger than it actually was. Rob was an incredible communicator and storyteller. In those days I couldn't imagine life without Rob and his family.

More mischief-making God lovers would join us over the course of those years. As I remember their faces, I am reminded of a statement written at the end of the movie *Stand By Me*, penned by Gordy, "I never had any friends like the ones I had when I was twelve... does anyone?" I would have to say an irrevocable *yes*.

The Spiritual Guide of Disappointment

In those days, Rob Morris's foundational message was that Jesus becomes a stumbling block to us, as He often was to His disciples. Often, Jesus becomes an offense to our flesh because He doesn't always live up to our expectations, Rob taught. I knew these unmet expectations first hand. I was 33 years old at the time and not married, and I held God responsible. I felt I was fulfilling His call on my life, and now He was disappointing me by not giving me what I felt I needed. *God you know I'll make a great husband and father,* I often thought. *Why not bless me with this? Haven't I been seeking Your Kingdom first?* These questions bombarded me as I was leading discipleship schools that were all about helping believers find their completeness and identity in Christ. Over the course of six months I realized I had a choice to make; I could react to this unmet expectation by becoming resentful, or I could trip over the stumbling block that is Jesus and allow a healthy sense of brokenness—a death to where I wanted to find my fulfillment.

One morning I remember sitting on a swing that was part of a play station in a little valley right below Trailer-Land. It was early evening and the golden rays of the autumn sun were casting their last beams through the foliage of the oak trees in front of me, illuminating a red dirt cloud that was following a vehicle as it drove by. I was holding the questions regarding my singleness before God as I pondered the words of Watchman Nee, "God will answer all your questions in one way and one way only, namely by showing you more of His Son."[50] A couple of minutes passed, and I became aware that I was more like Jesus than I thought. He was single when He walked this earth. He knew what I felt and could relate to my desires and questions.

In that moment my heart began to identify with His. No answers came, but I became aware of my union with Him and His enjoyment of me. We just swung together. Maybe this is what C.S. Lewis meant when he said, "Now I know Lord, why You give me no answer. Because You are Yourself the answer, and before Your face all questions die away." [51] For a moment I had an encounter with Him and everything else was suddenly extremely unimportant.

This encounter didn't mean that the questions would forever go away; they'd return in the months and years ahead. But somehow while I rocked on that swing I had befriended those questions. They were no longer my inner enemies.

The End of an Era

In 1995 Last Day Ministries closed as a community expression, and Melody Green and her then husband Andy Sievright moved to California to build what would become a web-based ministry. The property was sold to Ron Luce, the founder and director of Teenmania. As a pastoral team of friends, we fought long and hard to make the community expression of Last Days Ministries continue with Andy and Melody but to no avail. So, we spent the final months helping many of its staff find other ministries to join, and then sadly said goodbye to the dusty roads and magical memories of Trailer-Land and to our beloved community—though not entirely. My group of co-workers and friends could not un-belong to each other. We felt we had journeyed too far together in creating authentic community. Though we were not sure what to do next, we had become *God and us*, so we would not consider ministry options that didn't include us.

In the words of the British author, Tolkien, "All those who wander are not lost." [52]

In our wonderings and wanderings during the next six months we never felt lost, for we had found in each other our home.

Your Story

It takes practice to learn how to live well in the presence of eternal realities. The same is true for what Dietrich Bonhoeffer calls, *the Beloved Community*. Mother Teresa said, "If we have no peace it's because we have forgotten that we belong to one another." [53] To live in the awareness of what it means to belong to a community of faith, I will lead you through various rooms in what I call *the Beloved Community house*.

1. The first room of the Beloved Community house is history giving. It's essential that we make our life stories known as we journey with fellow believers. This week, practice openness with a friend and invite them into your spirituality of imperfection.

2. Venture into the second room of the Beloved Community house: commitment and confrontation. Pray for the friends with whom you have shared history. Are you holding any bitterness or forgiveness against someone? How can you affirm your commitment and support to that person this week?

3. Let's visit the second floor of the Beloved Community house and enjoy the rooms of playfulness and affirmation. The community that plays together stays together. Commit to a rhythm of recreation or entertainment with a close friend who is in need.

4. Make it a goal to give a word or act of encouragement to someone at least once a day, as the verse says, "Encourage one another while it is today" (Heb. 3:13). Write down the name of each person you encourage daily and pray for them before you go to bed.

*Communities of faith are those with whom you share Christ and a mutual mission.[54]

Notes

"The Eucharist needs to be a defining attitude, a way we meet life, receive it, and share it with others."

- Ronald Rolheiser, *Our One Great Act of Fidelity*

15

The Eucharist Life

"Let me make sure I understand you correctly," a Mercy Ship's staff friend said to me, rather perplexed. "You are considering moving your whole team up to New England to pioneer a new ministry in a place where none of you have ever lived before—right before Y2K hits?"

"Yes," I said in utter confidence, "Doesn't that sound exciting? We could really use you and your wife. You guys should consider joining us!"

After the Last Days Ministries community ended, the team and I moved to the Mercy Ship's center of operations just up the road. Don Stephens, it's president, graciously made room for us to develop discipleship training programs at their beautiful 440-acre property. All of us felt this was the best direction for our team, but a temporary one due to another vision that was taking shape in our hearts. Staying in east Texas made the transition easier for the families who had children in the local schools, and joining a stable ministry brought such healing after the disbanding of the Last Days Community.

During our three years at Mercy Ships we created a Discipleship Training School called The School of Christ, where we began to explore the contemplative life, incorporating silence and solitude into our prayer retreats. It was during this time that a vision stirred in our hearts for a new ministry in a different location. None of us were native Texans, so we felt no loyalty to stay in the state, and occasionally we felt like Texan culture was holding us hostage.

As we explored following Jesus as a way of life, we felt we needed a change of scenery, a different place to practice. Those of us who lived in Christian community were isolated from the marginalized and the orphaned. We also wanted to reach influencers, "the thinking man." We were smack in the middle of the Bible Belt, which meant the unchurched were very far away. The poor, the influencers, and the unchurched (or unsynagogued)—this broad swath of humanity—wasn't that who Jesus came to engage? We realized that we needed to consider moving to where they lived.

By 1998 our team had grown as we talked and dreamed together about creating an authentic community that revolved around two priorities: encounter and engagement. We interpreted this as loving God and loving others well. These were the values of the teams I lead to the Philippines, Hong Kong and Europe. Now my new community envisioned a ministry anchored in these same values. We longed for a Jesus-centered spiritual rhythm that would practice contemplative activism to reach the above-mentioned people.

Where should we go to fulfill this vision, we wondered? We were offered a facility in Santa Barbra, California (who wouldn't want to move there?) and other tempting options emerged. However, we were led to a part of the States where the attrition rate for new churches and ministries was five years and where we had few contacts and no invitations. It was the place that required the most trust: the northeast region of the States. With its educational, post-Christian bent, and a plethora of humanitarian needs, it seemed the perfect area.

After touring eight cities, we felt that New Haven, Connecticut, strategically located between Boston and New York City and home to

Yale University, would become an excellent place for us to pioneer what began as Youth With A Mission Axiom. (Axiom means "a self-evident indisputable truth.") We uprooted 25 people, mostly families, and left stable and defined ministries right before the feared Y2K (the date on which experts and pundits feared that computers worldwide might crash), to launch out on our great adventure.

A Home for Axiom

"It would be perfect if you could have your ministry headquarters down there in the Yale Ghetto," said Pastor Elander as he pointed to a cluster of old Victorian and Queen Anne homes beneath us. We were standing on the top of East Rock, a mountainous ridge that juts out of the New Haven landscape, the rugged majestic centerpiece of a 427-acre city park. It was a beautifully clear mid-August afternoon as Rick and Brenda Lewis, Jim Ehrman and I surveyed the quintessential New England city that stretched out before us, this town imbued with a mystique that rang from the gothic bell towers and cathedrals of Yale University. A humid breeze from the Long Island Sound, the grayish blue mass of water to our left, caused me to catch my breath for a moment as the wind stirred up dried leaves and candy wrappers at my feet.

Our hearts were equally stirred as Pastor Elander continued. "It would be a miracle for a house to come up for sale in that coveted neighborhood, but that's what you are believing for anyway, right?"

That moment of conversation and prayer on East Rock was another one of those *déjà vu* moments in my life. Everything felt oddly familiar in a wonderfully, nostalgic way as if we were living in a dream of God. So I'm not surprised when I look back and see how only a few months later not only one house, but two homes in the Yale Ghetto went up for sale. With further divine intervention we were able to purchase both. That was the beginning of a three-year season of favor, one in which all we put our hands and hearts to flourished.

We established a biblical worldview training school called "The Forum" that challenged and equipped believers to know what they believed. We started a seeker service, in partnership with a music venue called "The Space," led by Steve Rogers, and it drew the most eclectic group of people. Our hearts for the orphaned and marginalized—"the least of these"—erupted. Three international ministries were born: Love146, a charity dedicated to abolishing human trafficking and child-slavery; Streams of Mercy, Ten Thousand Homes, which built homes for orphan children in South Africa; and Child Restoration International, an organization that funds safe homes in India.

Our Spiritual Journey

During our first three years in New Haven, Connecticut a statement was given to us by a local Episcopal Priest that has been attributed to several saints, which helped shape our corporate pursuit of *following Jesus as a way of life,* "Ministry is effective only as it grows out of a current, intimate encounter with our Lord." We found that we had to commit to personal and corporate spiritual disciplines—what we would later call *a rhythm of formation*—in order to preserve our core value of encountering Jesus. Initially some people said this felt legalistic until we realized that if we didn't practice these commitments, we experienced little transformation in ourselves or in our community. Without the spiritual practices, we easily fell prey to busyness and spiritual burnout.

Parker Palmer said, "True community helps us reach towards wholeness, while reaching towards the world's needs, and trying to live at the intersection of the two." [55] Our goal as Axiom was to learn to live in this intersection. We committed to shared practices: participating in individual and corporate times of silence, solitude and prayer; partaking of the Eucharist weekly; practicing consistent acts of compassion and justice; and making our stories known to each other as well as to those who live without hope in this world.

We began to view our silence, solitude and prayer retreats not only as a precursor to ministry but also a fulfillment of the second commandment—a way of being lovingly present to each other in God. Some of my richest memories of those times were at the end of our afternoons in silence when we shared what we had experienced, sensed or heard.

However, when I look over the years of the existence of Axiom, the most meaningful times have been around the communion table. As I've seen the bread symbolically torn time and again, so have I watched courageous believers break open their lives: suicidal thoughts have been laid bare, dark secrets of abuse have refused their hiding places by crawling into the light, and pain-worn, sin-sick hearts have reached out in faith to touch the scars of the One who once whispered *by My wounds you are healed.*

With the pouring of the crimson wine of communion in various parts of the world, as Axiom participants we have seen gang members lay down their colors for reconciliation, a son and father become friends for the first time, and a marriage on the brink of divorce transformed into what the wife now calls, "a love that paints for me a picture of the face of Jesus every day."

Looking back on those moments where heaven touched earth in redemptive splendor has caused me to wonder, *is the Eucharist meant to be a mere ritual we participate in for momentary meaning or does it represent a gateway to a revolutionary way of life?* While pondering this question and participating in the practice in both traditional and creative ways, I've come to agree with Ronald Rolheiser's conclusion— "The Eucharist needs to be a defining attitude, a way we meet life, receive it, and share it with others. It needs to be a spirituality, namely, a way we undergo the presence of God and others in this world."[56]

As we continued to craft our Axiom communities, we explored what this kind of spirituality looked like. We embraced the four Eucharistic phrases Jesus gave us, and Rolheiser defined: receive, give thanks, break, and share.[57] At first these words appeared ever so simple and intriguingly child-like. But a closer look showed us the life-style implications of Jesus' challenge.

Isn't it countercultural in the world today to be vulnerable enough to be a perpetual learner, one who needs to always receive something? Doesn't this communicate weakness to others? To be grateful for whatever it is we receive and to break it and share it with others—this is foolishness to the world.

When I reflect upon our first ten-year journey as Axiom in New Haven, I've concluded that my personal successes and failures, as well as those of the ministry, can be defined by how well I lived out those four Eucharistic phrases. While using these phrases as a backdrop let's take a look at the Axiom history.

Receive

While we became established in New Haven we were excited about the location of our ministry homes. One was on Orange Street, one block from the base of East Rock Park. Orange Street represented what was often called the "townie-gownie divide." The "gownies," the wealthy and influential Yale students and faculty, lived on the west side of Orange Street, which was six blocks from the university. The "townies" lived on the east side of Orange, and ranged economically from the middle class to homeless. Thus, New Haven was a paradox of dichotomies: the extremely wealthy lived very close to the extremely poor. The financially challenged members of the community often roamed on the downtown Yale Green where U.S. Presidents like George Bush and wealthy businessmen have spoken, and where many famous musicians have played. But while New Haven is a hotbed for the training of influential leaders, lawyers, and artists, it also has one of the highest crime rates of any city in America.

While considering the dichotomies of our new home city, those of us who lived on Orange Street and Willow Street (one block from

Orange) knew *ministry* was right outside our front door. Mission was no longer a change of location. And since ministry is the affect our relationship with God has on others, we realized we needed to make intentional space for the encounter of that relationship to remain spiritually current and alive. We needed to make space to pause and receive.

As I studied the life of Jesus I was struck by what His life of encounter and engagement looked like as a contemplative activist. I was amazed at how and when He sought time with the Father hoping to receive something from Him. He sought an alone place before ministry and feeding the five thousand (Matt. 4:1-11), as well as after ministry (Matt. 14:23). He sought God before important decisions and the choosing of His twelve apostles (Luke 6:12). He withdrew to a solitary place when He was heart-broken after the beheading of John the Baptist (Matt. 1:35) and following a long night of work (Mark 1:35). After a joint mission with the twelve disciples He told them, "Come with me by yourselves to a quiet place and get some rest" (Mark 6:31). He felt that it was important to withdraw and be with the Father after healings (Luke 5:16) and as a retreat event when He took His disciples to the Mount of Transfiguration (Matt. 17:1-9). He also sought a quiet place to prepare for His highest work in the Garden of Gethsemane (John 26:36-46).[58]

Jesus, the very Son of God, was dependent on His Father for all that He needed. Could it be that we have no power to change ourselves or others outside what we have received from God?

I was blessed with a very gifted team of leaders who helped guide Axiom in those early years. We learned that when there are natural gifts, we don't always feel it a necessity to make space to receive; we can live in the illusion that what we have in and of ourselves is enough. And yet the Father repeatedly took us back to John 15: 5, "If you remain in me and I in you, you will bear much fruit, apart from me you can do nothing."

Give Thanks

The term Eucharist means gratitude, which is one of my sacred words. My most joyous moments have been when I have received a loving gift, when my heart is turned to gratitude for those gifts. The Eucharist is, of course, the grandest of these gifts.

Prior to arriving to New Haven there were moments when I had waited for externals to make me happy—a beautiful wife and family, a successful ministry, a ticket off the Alaskan crabbing boat. By placing joy in external possibilities, I postponed gratitude, which postponed true joy.

During a morning walk on the footpaths at the base of East Rock, I came to realize that this attitude communicated something to my Creator—I believed I deserved more than the gift of life, and intimacy with Him wasn't enough. But through Axiom, and in the years that followed, I've come to believe that the greatest gift we can give back to the Giver is the enjoyment of the gifts He's given us now, the communication of gratitude for those gifts. This is the kind of gratitude that changes our lives, but it can also change the lives of those around us.

Those who have left the holy fingerprints of God on my life have been those believers who walk in joy and gratitude. These people have viewed any good circumstances in their lives as mere icing on the cake but never the cake. Such a man I met briefly at Nelson Mandela's memorial service in Cape Town, South Africa, though we never exchanged a word.

I remember when I stepped forward to take communion at St. George's Cathedral, the Anglican Church from which Desmond Tutu presided, with Axiom Co-conspirator Steve Schallert.[59] As I knelt down at the front of the chapel and waited to be served, I suddenly felt the powerful presence of someone above me; I had rarely felt someone without first seeing them. I opened my eyes and looked up and was startled to see metal hook hands that carried the elements move slowly towards me. More penetrating than my awareness of the

Anglican Priest's silver hands and the burnt flesh scars on his face was the piercing look in his eye (one of his eyes didn't look real). It was as if he was pleading with me to understand the Eucharistic mystery— the pain, the love, the power of it all. His face glowed with an ecstatic grateful joy that has marked my life to this day. Despite unspeakable life circumstances, his joy overflowed. He was fully aware that he held and shared the treasure of all treasures.

Later I found he was a much loved and respected international advocate for reconciliation, forgiveness and restorative justice. His name was Father Michael Lapsley. After years of mobilizing faith communities worldwide to oppose apartheid and support the liberation struggle, and three months after Nelson Mandela's release from prison, the Civil Cooperation Bureau sent him a letter bomb. He lost both hands and the sight in one eye as the blast twisted and burned his body. It is said that while Father Michael was in the hospital, his greatest sadness was considering the possibility that he would not be able to serve the Eucharist anymore. [60]

I was the recipient of the life of the Eucharist from a man who knew he had *received* something from God and who *gave thanks* daily for the privilege he has in serving the body and blood of Jesus to others. I hope to fulfill the purpose of my creation—my activism— with equal gratitude and ecstatic joy.

Break

Buddhist spirituality suggests that almost everything that is wrong in the world can be explained in one image, that of the group photo. Whenever anyone looks at a group photo, the person invariably looks at how he or she turned out and only afterwards considers whether or not it is a good picture of the group. Breaking the Eucharist bread invites us to look first at how the group turned out. [61]

A Eucharistic person is one who calculates with the communal mind; one who is willing to break open narcissism, individualism, pride and all self-serving ambition for a greater freedom to love the whole of humanity. When we kept this kind of thinking and loving central as an Axiom community, we had much to share with the world. In those moments we learned to be together at the Eucharist table with our hurts, wounds, mistrust, bitterness, and suspicion and to exchange them for vulnerability, humility, forgiveness and reconciliation. When we didn't keep this proper breaking in exchange for goodness as a consistent practice, the beloved community stopped being the Beloved's.

In 2006, Axiom experienced a difficult season of transition where several of our partnering ministries began to evolve into their own organizations. Youth With A Mission had served as a good incubator for growth but could not contain the various visions that had emerged. What was both a painful and releasing process resulted in the new organizations becoming their own communities and the YWAM training arm of our mission continuing as a division of what became Axiom Monastic Community.

This transition produced a breaking that de-centralized Axiom and multiplied our efforts into various parts of the world. Did this breaking need to happen for multiplication to be possible? I would say yes. Bread is broken so that it can be distributed. But it is also broken to symbolize a way of life, an egoless spirituality we weren't willing to embrace at the time. Our eyes turned from the group photo and the face of the One who breaks what he takes, and thus I wonder if God initiated the manner in which we were ultimately broken.

I experienced the greatest sadness with those who had been together since Last Day Ministries. We realized that we were no longer going to grow old and grey together as we had hoped and that our breaking meant we would have to stop belonging to each other.

Nonetheless, we've learned that a Eucharistic spirituality invites us to imitate Christ's sacrifice, the letting Himself be broken and emptied for no other reason but that of love.

Share

"The place God calls you to," said Frederick Buechner, "is the place where your deep gladness and the world's deep hunger meet."[62] During my first few years pioneering Axiom in New England, I was in pursuit of finding this meeting place and felt it would somehow involve the poor. I knew I had received much, and I wanted a greater avenue to share myself, to love much. Through conversations with dear friends in England and scripture study, I was captured by the realization that Jesus referred to the poor as his family, so I began to ask God two questions. *How can your family be a greater part of my life? You have adopted me into your family; how could I adopt yours into mine?*

I didn't think he'd take my question literally.

God's greatest gift to me—the best opportunity to share myself—showed up at my front door on May 5, 2001. Before I met Brandon and Patrick when they were seven and eight years old, I was aching to be a father. I had joked around with a friend and said, "If I'm not married by forty I'll just adopt some kids if I can somehow skip the diaper phase!" God must have heard my request. The big forty arrived, and so did my sons.

In New Haven I couldn't have asked for a better community to come alongside me and share the experience of parenting. I learned that we can receive, give thanks, and break, but if this isn't followed by sharing, often in the context of community, our joy isn't complete. We are not passing on the legacy of lessons learned from our struggles as well as our joys.

I was so excited to share my children with my family. Mom and Dad met Brandon and Patrick at the SeaTac airport, Washington, for our first of many Christmas holidays with them on Whidbey Island. Tim and Becky, who lived near my parents, already had kids my sons' ages, which made for a quick natural fit for the new cousins.

Even after the years passed into 2010 and Mom's short-term memory was fading away, I felt as if Brandon and Patrick had always been part of the family; they stayed firmly in her mind. I remember the day she heard Patrick would be attending a Snowboarders YWAM Discipleship Training School; she asked me three times in one afternoon, "When will Patrick be leaving for his DTS? He won't be missing Christmas with us, will he?" I didn't mind answering her over and over again because it reminded me that with all that she wouldn't remember in the years ahead, Mom would never forget how to love.

While being raised a Mormon I remember fearing that someday I would be judged for the things I'd done right or wrong in this life. I think St. John of the Cross had the truer assessment of what will be most important to God: "In the evening of our lives we'll be judged by our loving." [63]

I remember one gathering service when my sons' biological mother surprised me and showed up while I was speaking. I changed my message immediately and began to talk about how there was someone in the audience who was very much like God.

"How?" I asked, "God knows what it's like to give up that which was most precious out of love," I said. "He gave up His son so he could *share* Himself with us and show us that in the giving of life not in the hoarding of it we are most free. I want to publicly thank this mother who did a similar courageous act," I said. "In giving up her sons Brandon and Patrick she has somehow rescued me."

Your Story

I suggest that the Eucharist is not a mere ritual we participate in for momentary meaning, but it represents a gateway to a revolutionary life— a way of engaging with the presence of God and others in the world.[64] Let's reflect on the four Eucharist phrases Jesus gave us with practices that will lead us into the Eucharist life.

1. *Receive and Give Thanks* – After you wake up in the morning, consciously make space to receive something from God, then journal what He has given you. Before you go to bed at night make a list of all the ways God has blessed you throughout the day, followed by a time of worship and thanksgiving.

2. *Break and Share* - Come to the Eucharist table this week with any hurts, wounds, mistrust, bitterness, or suspicion and practice breaking in exchange for goodness. Exchange whatever burden or negative attitude you are carrying for vulnerability, humility, or forgiveness and reconciliation. Then give what you need. If you lack encouragement and support, give encouragement and support. If you lack finances, share what you have.

3. Read the following condensed version of a contemplative exercise, written by Anthony De Mellow, called *The Awakening*. Read his words slowly and allow the Spirit to guide your mental imagery as you enter into the practice of gratefulness.

"I make believe that I am paralyzed from the shoulders down. I vividly imagine my surroundings and notice what my thoughts and feelings are. I see the changes paralysis has brought about in my work and profession, my relationships, my self-image, my relationship with God, my views on life. I contemplate an average day, from the moment of my waking in the morning till I fall asleep at night: my first thoughts upon awaking, my meals, my work, my toilet needs and therapy, my entertainment and prayer.

"At night I dedicate some minutes in thanksgiving. I am thankful for the gift of speech: I can express my needs and feelings, I can relate to others, even help them. And hearing: I can hear the sound of music and the song of birds and human voices.

"And sight: I can look at flowers and trees, and stars at night and the faces of my friends. I am full of gratitude for taste, smell, touch, thought, memory, fantasy, and feeling. And now the time has come to be grateful for paralysis itself: I look at the blessing it has brought till I can see it as a gift. If I can bring myself to do this I will have tasted a moment of the purest mysticism, namely, of an acceptance of everything that is.

"I now reflect on something in my life that I resent, resist: a physical defect, an illness, and unavoidable situation, a circumstance I live in, a happening of the past, a person. And, step-by-step I do with it what I did with my 'paralysis.' So that, without relinquishing my desire and efforts to get rid of it if possible, I bring myself to gratitude for it, for everything, for every single thing."[65]

Notes

*"Give thanks in all circumstances; for this is God's will
for you in Christ Jesus."*

-1 Thessalonians 5:18

"We must begin to care for creation, for humanity and for the divine sparks of divinity in every aspect of life."

- John Howard Yoder, And We Will Become a Happy Ending

16

Body, Mind, Spirit

I could see the reflection of a Mormon missionary in the window of our living room while he knocked on the door of our Willow Street house in New Haven, Connecticut. *Where was his partner?* I wondered, remembering that I had met them on the Yale Green a couple of days ago. I stepped onto the front porch to greet him, and after shaking hands and exchanging niceties he said, "When you spoke to us about Jesus the other day, it's as if you really knew Him. Then last night I saw your community at the soup kitchen having fun and serving the people. It's all made me interested in knowing more about your faith. Do you have a couple minutes to talk?"

"Sure," I said, and invited him in to join our Eucharist service that was being set up at that moment. While he followed me he said, "Us Mormons are taught that when the true gospel of Mormonism was restored to the world through Joseph Smith that all other churches were an abomination to God. I just can't believe that anymore." [66]

It was 2008, two years after the dispersion of most of the Axiom Community. One of our ministries had moved on to South Africa and another stayed in New Haven and became a charity. Some Axiom families were still working on selling their homes so they could live closer to relatives or in a cheaper part of the States. I was overseeing the Youth With A Mission staff in New Haven and those who wanted to continue to pursue our original goal—following Jesus as a way of life.

That morning, while the Mormon missionary joined us for communion, I began to recite John's account of the events that happened right after Jesus' death and resurrection.

"The disciples didn't know that the man building a fire on the shore while they were fishing was Jesus," I said. "Perceived as a stranger, He guided them to cast their net into a perfect place for an abundant catch."

I paused for a moment and looked at the weary faces of those around the table. Everyone looked so emotionally spent, the byproduct of the long season of transition in Axiom.

"Does anyone remember when the disciples finally recognized it was Jesus on the shore?" I asked. I was met with blank stares.

"It's when Jesus spoke some of my favorite words 'Come to Breakfast.'" I surveyed the room, then continued, "Though the disciples didn't recognize Jesus at first, they were familiar with His voice of love and His perpetual invitation to sit down and feed them. A few verses later before asking Peter, 'Do you love me,' and commissioning him into an active faith, Jesus wanted Peter to come and receive first—come and be loved."

My new Mormon missionary friend broke the silence.

"I don't know a Jesus like that," he said. "All my life I've been trying to answer Jesus' question, 'Do you love me?' by working to please Him and become a god someday. I don't even know how to do what you said—to come and receive, to come and be loved."

"Well, let's learn together," I said, "here around the Eucharist table, and then out in the world. This experience of receiving love, and then giving it away, is the heart of what it means to follow Jesus, to become a contemplative activist. That's our aspiration—a journey where we will always be perpetual learners."

Several others added their affirming thoughts, and after sharing communion together, we prepared to walk individually to the Yale Green and practice this receiving and giving life. We wanted to hold before our spiritual eyes the realization we had been discussing the past month—God communes with us through interaction with the things closest to Jesus' heart: the poor, the widow, the outsider, creation, and children.

Before we departed, my Mormon missionary friend had to leave to meet up with his partner, but he wanted to get together in the evening to hear of my experience.

My Contemplative Walk

A man who was homeless approached me with a gentle smile and asked for some change on the Yale Green in downtown New Haven. I quickly looked away from him and wondered if I should stop. *There are many homeless people in the area,* I thought. *You can't stop for everyone.* I smelled beer when he walked by. *That's probably what he'll spend my money on.* I kept walking and felt good about my decision.

A stranger approached me asking for directions. After helping her for a moment I could tell she just needed a listening ear, so I sat down with her on a park bench, and we talked for a while. In that moment, God gave Himself to me and blessed me with the reward of loving another.

I stopped by Trinity on the Green Episcopal Church to meet a friend. To my surprise I noticed the homeless man I had passed on the street earlier. He was kneeling on one of the benches praying. He had a crumpled handkerchief in one of his hands that he used to dry the tears that were rolling down the deep wrinkles of his cheeks. Clutched in his other hand tightly, as if it were his only source of sustenance, was a small crucifix. He stared at it like he was looking at an old faithful wife who loved him more than she could ever say. I was deeply moved by the expression on his face and felt guilty for not having responded to his needs. My mistake was clear; I'd preferred the put-together wanderer over the homeless man. *Who we are inside determines what we see. What we see determines what we do,* I thought. Conviction was immediate.

When we embrace the life of contemplative activism, our mistakes become our faithful teachers as we learn to pay attention to what is most important to God.

During my first fifteen years of being a Christian, I was very particular and limited in how I allowed God to give Himself to me, and in return, how I chose to give myself back to Him. I thought, dualistically: *If I don't agree with your theology, I can't learn from you. I can't learn from the earth because that's too New Age. I can't learn from those who aren't Christian because what do they have to offer? I can't learn from Catholics because they pray with the saints and Mary. If I give too much attention to what I perceived as the liberal agenda: the poor, issues of social justice, and creation, I'd be wasting my time with nonessentials.* Fast-forward 15 years—and many lessons on humility later—and all of life has become my teacher.

A New Monasticism

As Axiom Community, we've been attempting to answer one question: How can we effectively be God's real presence in the world? During our years of transition and re-evaluation we felt led to explore what has been called an ancient-future spirituality. It is ancient in that we learn from the wisdom traditions and the many cloud of witnesses who have gone before us, and it is future in that we take responsibility to assimilate the truths that God is entrusting to His people in this day and age. This distinct spirituality can be referred to as a *new monasticism.*

In the Axiom years, we were excited to discover that many individuals and communities around the world were banding together to live out their Christian lives with greater intention and to explore a radical whole-life faith. "I believe there is a Creator, a revolutionary force at work that is compelling us towards love, health and wholeness," said John Howard Yoder. "We must begin to care for creation, for humanity and for the divine sparks of divinity in every aspect of life. We must accept the invitation to work with God in His redeeming story, Jesus' story, our story, the story."[67] New Monastic communities tend to the divine sparks of divinity that undergird and advance the Kingdom of God in the following ways: nurturing a common community life and shared economy; peacemaking and reconciliation; caring for creation, and the maturing of its members through contemplative practices. We felt that to pursue these objectives more fully was to be our next Axiom mission.

Rhythms of Formation

With the start of 2010, we decided as a community that it was time to examine our rhythms of life, a phrase that refers to how we go about getting our daily needs and desires met. To embrace a radical, whole-life faith, we adapted a rhythm of formation so that "Christ may be formed in us" (Gal. 4:19). We've come to believe this is a holistic involvement of spirit, mind and body.

Drawing upon an ancient-spirituality, we examined how the Christ-followers of the past referred to a rule of life as their rhythm of formation. This term meant doing life in such a way that members were anchored and centered in the love of God through practicing the spiritual disciplines and spreading them throughout the day and week. Having touch-points with God, and through loving attentive pauses, we begin to experience a true love relationship. In these experiences we practice being fully present to Him and to the needs of those around us.

What has informed the nature of our rule of Life for Axiom in the past five years has been a future spirituality, which God has been showing His followers recently regarding preparedness. The fields of neuroscience and the practices of mindfulness, body attunement and sustainable living have experienced major advancements. Recent studies have shown how we can respond to the negative experiences of our past in a positive manner through practices that rewire the neural networks of our mind. This rewiring initiates a healing journey that releases fresh hope that directly affects our physical bodies. We have been exploring these arenas in daily practice as well as through our The Integrated Mind Retreat so that we can faithfully steward our thought lives, which affect the flesh and bone containers they come in.

Anyone who knows me knows that I'm a foodie. My dream day is when I'm able to arrange my meals around foods from countries that border the Mediterranean Sea. I've also seen how the foods I eat, along with physical exercise, directly affects my clarity of mind and influences how I engage with God and the world around me. Though I periodically change my rhythm of formation according to my personal needs, that rhythm always involves at least 150 minutes a week of mild aerobic activity, fasting (which I once hated), and if available— popcorn with a good movie.

What's Worthy of Our Time?

Many of us live in a culture that is losing its grip on God's redeeming story, a culture captivated by a very different narrative: the right to happiness. When we first experimented with rhythms of formation at Axiom, many of us realized we had unconsciously fallen prey to this narrative. We had found that the way we spent our hours or days was mainly to secure our comfort, financial security, and social status. We were living for temporary happiness. We loved the idea of following Jesus as a way of life, but to actually follow Him daily through rhythms of formation was initially difficult.

Don't the most valuable things in life cost time and effort?

And listening to my story, you may be considering a whole-life faith and thinking: *My life is already too busy without adding more to my to-do list.* The purpose of rhythms of formation isn't to fill our lives with more activities but to fill our activities with *more love.* Through Axiom, I learned that adopting a rhythm of slowing down and listening, of re-evaluating my day while it is happening, allows me to be more loving and present to the needs of the moment. In other words, only when I'm resting in my deep center and cultivating an authentic inner world with Christ can I live effectively in my outer world. This lifestyle of being at home with God, "in whom we live and move and have our being," [68] is the only spiritual reality that enables me to be of service to others for the long haul.

To give shape to this way of doing life, I live by the mantra "less is more." In implementing formational practices I begin by making slight adjustments within my already established rhythm of life that is natural to how I eat, work, and sleep. I'm a morning person, so my daily quality time of prayer and body exercise has always been right after I wake up. However, I don't go to the Internet until my morning rhythms are finished. I avoid the Internet an hour before I go to bed at night. I do this because I enjoy starting and ending my day with an uncluttered mind, meditating on the truths that God has highlighted in my life.

Before going to bed at night I enjoy a version of "The Prayer of Examen." [69] I reflect upon my day with God to see what I have learned, where have I loved, and how I can be true to my call as a follower of Jesus.

After lunch during the work week, I have an intercessory prayer time, usually in public areas like city parks or train stations. This rhythm sustains daily evangelism and my mission as "monastery on the road," where I listen to the heartbeat of God wherever I find myself.[70] This time is prolonged on Thursdays, which is my weekly day of fasting and the day on which I slip into an afternoon time of silence and solitude.

On weekends, when the ocean is accessible and agreeable, I recapture my love for surfing—a reminder to me of how beautifully the mind, body and spirit can work together to properly catch a wave. This act mirrors to me how, through stillness and letting go, I can position my heart and mind to embrace the ever-present movements of God and the prayers of His people.

While I live my rhythms, I realize that my God gives Himself to me in ordinary days and ways. These rhythms teach me that I have the ultimate privilege of receiving and then giving.

A Lost Son

After Axiom's transitional years, another difficult time in my life emerged as I watched my son Brandon—who had once sat on my shoulders—turn to substance abuse to ease the pain that had surfaced in his life. Prior to this, we had one of the closest relationships I had ever witnessed between a father and a son, and he had become the joy of my heart. It wasn't the rhythms of formation that saved me from those challenging six years, but it was the grace, comfort and identification the Lord gave me through the practices. Let me explain.

Geoff Little, a friend of mine, recounted a story from his pulpit about a man who had to hospitalize his wife because of the severity of her Alzheimer's condition. Every day he would visit her at two in the afternoon—that was his rhythm of love with her. One day his medical appointment was going longer than expected. He told the doctor, "I need to leave in a couple minutes or I will be late for my time with my wife."

The doctor said, "I don't mean to be irreverent, but your wife will not know if you're late. She doesn't even recognize you anymore."

"That's true doctor," he conceded, "but although she doesn't know me anymore, I know and love her, and I live for those lucid moments in which, maybe once or twice a year, she mentally wakens. During those times, I sit beside her on her hospital bed, and we talk for hours about our lives together, our wedding day, our wonderful children, and the good and hard times. Then suddenly, without notice, she drifts away. Doctor, I have to go—this could be the day that she awakens, and I don't want to miss one lucid moment with her; I love her too much for that."

What was the grace that sustained me when Brandon would come home late at night drunk, wondering if life was worth living? It was the knowledge that there was a God who lived for lucid moments with me. As I learned how to be fully present to Him in my pain, with my questions, I became aware of the constancy of His moment-by-moment visitations. I became aware of how the Father of all fathers feels when His prodigal sons and daughters have chosen to no longer live at home. I learned that waiting is often the hardest work of hope.[71]

Your Story

Science affirms that what we do with our minds affect our bodies and vice versa. Thus let's consider several reflective questions and spiritual exercises that will help us discover what rhythms of formation will bring our whole self into alignment. Let's *live ourselves into a new way of thinking,*[72] and recognize the One who is always giving Himself to us.

1. Find a quiet place with God where there are no distractions. Consider how your body is the temple of the Holy Spirit (1 Cor. 6:19). What is your body telling you about what you need? Is there a rhythm of formation regarding your body that will help you be a better steward of your whole self? Maybe a weekly fast, healthier desserts, or 150 minutes of aerobic exercise a week?

2. Go to your village or city center and have a *contemplative walk.* Your goal as you walk and pray is to have spiritual eyes that see the many ways God is choosing to give Himself to you. Pay particular attention to the biases of His son: the poor, the widow, the outsider, and creation. Make it your pleasure to give back to Him in a way that is a natural outflow of your love for Him and others.

3. Turn to the Appendix of this book (pg. 265) and establish or revise your rhythm of formation according to the needs of your body, mind and spirit—where you are being challenged as an aspiring contemplative activist. Keep in mind that *less is more.*

Notes

"The future will be judged by our capacity to re-wild our spirituality, standing on the shoulders of the past, yes, but walking with our eyes on the dawn rising."

- Reverend Johnny Sertin

17

Eternity is Now

"You are preparing them to be released from captivity?" I asked the Zimbabwean as I suspiciously eyed the two lionesses that would accompany me on an hour walk across the savannah.

"Yes," said the guide who would be watching us from a distance.

"But are they not wild yet?" I questioned.

"Some say lions never stop being wild," he replied with no hint of encouragement, "they just act tame when they are in captivity."

"I suppose they will put on a good act during my walk with them right?" I asked, then added that I wouldn't be paying him until it was over.

I was instructed which lioness I could touch on the back and which one I couldn't—the one that was almost ready to be released from captivity. Both walked slowly on my left with the swagger of the Pink Panther, and I, with less confidence, began to follow the guide down the trail.

For the next forty-five minutes we had an enchanting walk. The tame lioness occasionally plopped herself down in front of my legs as if she wanted to be petted. She did this mid-stride, almost causing me

to trip over her on several occasions. The guide abruptly tapped her
with a stick, instructing her not be so friendly. The walk was pleas-
antly uneventful until we stopped to take a photo on a large rock. In
French, the guide counted to three. Right when I smiled and laid my
hand on the tame lioness's back, she snapped at my arm! I moved just
fast enough to escape her bite.

Thus, our photo session ended.

"She must be tired or irritated," the guide explained as he jogged
to where I stood and guided the lions away from me.

"Or hungry!" I added, almost breathless.

"You have to be alert," he instructed, as if I had done something
wrong. "This is typical of lions," he continued. "They will walk slowly
alongside you for a long time and become almost unnoticeable, and
you will think they are just a big house cat. Then, once you let your
guard down, once you turn to the beauty of the landscape, you become
vulnerable to their attack."

Knowing Our Enemy

Sometimes I think we give Satan too much attention. Sometimes
we blame the devil for things that are our own fault. That doesn't
mean I haven't seen him as a player in my life, often present and unnoticeable. Rather, I have found him to be very consistent. He whispers
in my ear, tells me only a sliver of the truth, and entices me with the
promise of immediate gratification. He consistently lies to me about
where true life is found. His strategy is to keep me from living at home
with God and His beloved community.

Peter writes, "be self-controlled and alert. Your enemy the devil
prowls around like a roaring lion looking for someone to devour"
(1 Peter 5:8). This verse and my life bear testimony to the fact that
the only way the enemy is like God is that he is a pursuer. He is *looking*
for someone to devour, but God is *looking* for "those whose hearts

are completely His, so He may fully support Him" (2 Chron. 16:9, NASB). The opposite of being self-controlled and alert is being mindless and undisciplined. When I adopt the later postures, I'm the most vulnerable to the enemy's bite. That's why I need rhythms of formation in my life, rhythms that help me be alert and pay attention.

The enemy knows that the only place we have peace and power is right here, right now. Eternal life is to be aware of, and remain in union with, the *I am* God of this present moment; that is the heart of contemplation. This truth is confirmed in John 17:3, "Now this is eternal life that they may know you, the only true God, and Jesus Christ, whom you have sent."

The Pilgrimage Life

After my incident with the lions in Zimbabwe, I thought I would go play kick ball with the elephants, my new favorite animal. I once thought that because they were so big they must also be stupid. This is far from the case. Elephants are ingenious in how they protect their newborn and how they herd. Did you know there is even an elephant that can paint profiles of people while holding a paintbrush in his trunk?

My friend Jerry and I felt like circus roadies as our guides had us climb on the elephants' backs and sit on their knees while they performed tricks. After we had relaxed with these beautiful creatures, one of the guides asked me, "Where is your home?" He hadn't asked me, "Where are you from?" which would have been easier to answer.

"New Haven, Connecticut, has been my most recent home," I responded, "It's an hour and a half north of New York city on the northeast coast of the States."

"But where is your home now?" he asked, actually interested.

"I'm living the life of a pilgrim at the moment," I answered, knowing that he would require an explanation of this as well. He was a

Christian, so I continued, "My sons are in their early twenties, living on their own. My call for this season of life is to live as a church without walls," I said, "living openly amongst unbelievers and believers in a way that the life of God in me can be seen, challenged, and questioned."[73]

"Like Jesus lived with his disciples, huh?" He responded.

"I seek an encounter with God through the people and situations I meet along the way. I try to serve, listen and love. Sometimes I do this successfully, sometimes not," I explained.

"Wow, that sounds fun! Better than only going to church I think," he replied.

"Yes it's fun and adventurous at times," I said with some apprehension, "but it's also a voluntary exile. Sometimes I yearn for the familiar, my old pillow," I continued, "for the physical home I once had. But this is my mission for now. In the places I go to, in these new 'dark ages,' I can see that the people I meet along the way are also yearning for home." [74] He continued to stare in amazement at me. "As you and I know the stability of this wild journey is the home found in Christ and a heart anchored in His love."

Before embarking on my own personal pilgrimage in 2012, a network of Axiom communities, individual participants, and apprentices began to emerge around the world. Our uniting bond became a shared rhythm of formation and the three "E's" that capture our mission to the world: encountering Christ, enriching cultures, and emancipating the oppressed. We lived a life of pilgrimage as Axiom members, remembering that "Blessed are those who strength is in You and have set their hearts on Pilgrimage" (Psalm 84:5). In our travels we encountered spiritual seekers who had been disillusioned by the institutional church, but who had a hunger for something more—even more of Jesus than they were finding among their Christian friends. Some of these seekers were led by this hunger to hit the road, to seek for truth outside themselves. And this commitment to pilgrimage kept calling us back to a continual seeking, to refusing to give into settling for the comfort of easy answers that contemporary culture offers us.

Ian Morgan Cron captures the yearning of pilgrimage well in his book entitled *Chasing Francis* when he says, "A Pilgrimage is a way of praying with your feet. You go on a pilgrimage because you know there's something missing inside your soul, and the only way you can find it is to go to sacred places, where God made Himself known to others. In sacred places, something gets done that you've been unable to do for yourself." [75]

Burning Hearts and Re-Wilding

As Axiom we've discovered that the story of the disciples on the road to Emmaus is an excellent template for pilgrimage. Two of the disciples walked with Christ, not recognizing Him after the resurrection. At the end of that walk, which involved conversation, questions, and learning together, they broke bread in their home and the disciples received the revelation about the identity of their companion. As they later discussed their journey with Jesus they said, "Did not our hearts burn within us" (Luke 24:32)?

Pilgrimage sets us out in anticipation of revelation. On pilgrimage, we look for our place of resurrection, a continual conversion of self and the world we live in. In that place, God sometimes answers our questions, and other times He questions our answers.

To have our hearts set on pilgrimage has to do with making space for unfamiliar people and unfamiliar places in our lives. Before embracing the life of a pilgrim three years ago, I found that I had been gravitating towards the familiar again, which gave me a greater sense of control and safety. I had chosen speaking engagements and mission trips to those places where little risk was involved. My eyes became open when I realized that my heart no longer burned with the raw passion and faith that it once had. I knew I needed to hit the road again to get out of my comfort zone and to seek the burning bush of His presence among the unknown. I felt God would be waiting for me there in the unknown, and in that place my heart would be set aflame once again.

The country of Zimbabwe has been involved with the task of re-wilding animals. It is the practice of returning areas of land to their natural, wild state. I believe the ancient –future spirituality we've been exploring with the contemplative practices has a similar purpose. How? God has chosen to hide Himself among the poor, the stranger, the unfamiliar, the soil of the earth, and the high hard places of land and sea as the Celts discovered, so that only those who want to follow Him as a way of life will be able to truly find Him, and re-wild the state of their hearts.

Zimbabwe became one of my frontiers of fresh exploration. I had never been there and had only one contact in a nation of great need. This contact, Jerry Johnson, was an old friend who had been with me on my first amazing trip to Subic Bay in the Philippines. He now worked with Oasis, a Christian Charity and anti-trafficking movement, and he invited me to come and run a retreat for their staff. After two weeks in this wonderful nation, Jerry, two of his local friends and I went to downtown Harare to assess the needs of the street children.

We arrived at an old, out of service, dilapidated bus station filled with large mounds of garbage every few yards. There were small, barely tended street fires where homeless families were gathered. I remember that we needed to be careful where we stepped as we made our way around the refuse cluttered mud puddles to where the children were playing. One jolly little guy with an amazingly deep giggle immediately ran up to me and began to run his hands through the hair on my arms. When I started to talk to him, a drunken man who had been singing behind one of the garbage mounds stepped out from the shadows and yelled at me. I ignored him and continued to chat with my new little friend.

Suddenly, the drunken man pushed himself between us and said, "Pray for me!" My first thoughts were not, *sure I'd love to.* I wanted to tell him to go and bother someone else so I could give my full attention to the children. But I couldn't bring myself to say, "No, I don't want to pray for you." So, I quickly put my hand on his shoulder and blurted out what I would call a courtesy prayer.

When I had said "Amen," to my shock the man had become completely sober and in a voice of urgent authority he added, "I must lead you to your car right now. You must go." My friend Jerry heard his request as well, and we grabbed our two local friends and casually accompanied the man to our car. I felt God's presence tangibly in that moment and my heart burned within me. Once we unlocked the doors of the car, got inside and locked them, rocks and bricks began to smash into our vehicle! We tried to drive forward but there was a large, violent crowd of people who began throwing stones at us. We pulled a U-turn and peeled out. While looking through our back windows we could see people chasing us and screaming with wild, violent looks in their eyes. Later we discovered that they had thought we were conspiring against the government. Their plan had been to kill us.

I'm glad that I prayed for that man and didn't follow my ego! This event confirmed to me that I was walking in stride with the Wild One again, and the burning bush of God's presence was aflame with power and purpose amongst unfamiliar people and unfamiliar places.

Is it possible that we have domesticated Christianity to the point where the untamable God no longer feels at home within our controlled, religious hearts? My friend, Johnny Sertin, who had stood with me at the crumbling Berlin wall in 1987 said, "The answer is not retreating into mirroring past traditions or rearranging current ecclesiastical furniture. The future will be judged by our capacity to re-wild our spirituality, standing on the shoulders of the past, yes, but walking with our eyes on the dawn rising." [76]

St. Francis and Acts of Protest

In the spring of 2010, after teaching at a YWAM center in Amsterdam, I followed a desire of my heart to an unfamiliar place I had always longed to explore: the birthplace of St. Francis of Assisi in Italy. Without one contact or knowing any Italian, I ventured to one of Europe's best-preserved medieval cities in the hill country of Umbria.

On a dark night during a spring storm, and very weary from a busy teaching week, I fell asleep quickly in a quaint little hotel in Assisi. When I awoke, I felt a breeze coming through the window I had left open the night before. The breeze carried the sweet smell of freshly cooked pastries and the sound of sparrows playing as they made their circular dives off the edge of my balcony. Noticing the striking land-scape through my window, I stood reverently to my feet as I became aware of where I was. The Umbria plains spread beneath me, a golden patchwork quilt of sunflowers fields and farmlands, peppered with clumps of dark green foliage and pointed, stately cypress trees. The ancient chapel torrents and bell towers of Assisi framed the view—I took in a deep breath of wonder, wanting to inhale all the enchantment before my eyes. *Francis, this is why it was so easy for you to find God here amongst His creation,* I thought.

Half an hour later, I roamed the cobbled streets and corridors of lower Assisi. It all seemed magically familiar as if I were once again walking out a dream God had planned for me long ago. *Considering the yearning in my younger years to have lived in the medieval era,* I thought, *how apropos for my spiritual journey to bring me to this place to learn from those who lived for God back then.*

While I paused in the Piazza S. Pietro to listen to a European youth orchestra, one of its cello players, a young man from Poland, walked up to me, introduced himself, and said, "We will be playing a mini-concert to welcome the sunrise in the enclaves of Rocca Maggiore castle that sits at the top of the hill on which Assisi is built. We are afraid that we will have no audience because it is scheduled so early in the morning. Would you mind coming so we can play for you?"

"It would be an honor," I said immediately struck by such an opportunity. "Which morning?"

"I think Tuesday," he said.

"I'll be there," I said. *What a phenomenal experience,* I thought, *to hear a live 75-person orchestra play in such a breathtaking location, just for me!*

Tuesday morning arrived. I quickly showered to jolt myself into the reality of the 5:00 am hour. I hurriedly made my way through the medieval maze of alleyways that led up to the castle. Without anyone in sight, there was no sign that I was in the 21-century. It felt like I was a knight on a secret mission. As I ascended staircase after staircase my rapidly thumping heart seemed so loud that anyone could hear it. *Where is the top?* I wondered. *They said it was just a fifteen-minute ascent.* It was, but the steep grade made it feel so much longer. Nevertheless, I quickened my pace. *If I am their only audience,* I thought, *I don't want to be late.*

When I finally reached the top of the hill, there stood the weathered but solid stonewall of the castle. I was struck by the silence that hung in the air. *Shouldn't I hear the orchestra warming up,* I wondered? *It doesn't sound like a large group of young people is waiting behind those walls.* I walked up to the gigantic gate, and to my grave disappointment it was locked. I peered through a crack in the wall and the enclave was empty, not a person in sight! *How sad,* I thought, *I got up early to climb all the way up here for nothing. What a waste!* Then, I turned around and froze as my eyes fell upon the view. *A waste,* I thought, *in the presence of such beauty?*

The sleepy ramparts, domes, and church steeples of Assisi were all below. Stretching to my right and to my left were the shadowed plains of Umbria, an enormous lavender tapestry speckled with little twinkling lights as far as the eyes could see. In awe and reverence, I found a place beside the crumbling walls of the castle and watched the sun rise between the mountains.

God tricked me in coming up here, I thought, *so that He could have my full attention.*

After a while I took my Bible out of my backpack and I read, "Blessed is the man who listens to me, watching daily at my doors, waiting at my doorway. For whoever finds me finds life and receives favor from the Lord" (Prov. 8:34). *What a promise, to have God's favor and to find life,* I thought. So I prayed: *Lord, I'm going to come every morning for the sunrise while I'm here in Assisi and watch daily at Your doorway.*

My last morning in wondrous Assisi had come too soon. My muscles were sore from hiking the day before, so when the alarm clock sounded at 5:15, I stared, wondering if it really mattered if I missed one morning. *But I made a promise,* I thought, and I remembered that the role of the enemy is to rob, steal and destroy. So I threw on my clothes, rushed out of the hotel, and sprinted through the alleyways knowing I already had a late start. The sky above me was readying itself for the first beams of light, beams that would chase away the great shadow of Mount Sabasio from the city and the plains below. *I have to get there on time,* I thought, *my last morning in Assisi!* Though my legs were shaking and sweat was trickling down my chest, I forced myself to jog up the last painful flight of stairs. Once at the top when the castle was in view, I suddenly heard a trumpet. Then a fleet of violins ascended into the brisk morning air. *What?* I thought, *the orchestra is here, now! The Polish guy must have told me the wrong day!*

I ran to the open gate and stepped into the enclave. There filling the hollow of the castle was the orchestra. The sun was about to rise; they were waiting and didn't want to start without me. Once they saw I had arrived, they began to play "On Earth As It Is In Heaven" best known from the movie, *The Mission.* The sun seemed to have been waiting also and could no longer hold back her beams. With a great yawn, she stretched her golden fingers out into the sky.

I was so overwhelmed by the shocking beauty of all that was before me I had to lean against the castle wall to maintain my balance. *I can't believe I almost missed this most spectacular of moments,* I thought! Then I instantly remembered what the Lord had spoken to me the first morning I had been there: God's favor and blessing is with those who watch, wait and are ready now for His coming in the moment, and for His future coming. "The virgins who were ready went in with him to the banquet" (Matt. 24:10).

A Theology of Revolt

I believe there will be a time in the future when the divine trumpet will sound and it will be too late to spiritually prepare for what is to come. The global, economic and political climate will be so chaotic and confusing that only those who have been watchful, who have prepared their hearts and minds will know how to respond well, and if necessary, to suffer well.

However, I don't believe we are to watch and wait passively. We are to be acutely aware that there is an enemy who wants to convince us that we don't live in what C.S. Lewis calls *a universe at war,* and therefore righteous acts are not needed.[77] The enemy's theology is that of resignation while authentic Christianity is a theology of revolt—of protest. Our contemplative practices are literal acts of protest against the wiles of the enemy and our consumerist, narcissistic culture. When we create a quiet place in an urban center to till the soil, to plant, to pray, it's an act of protest against the falsehood that the world is ours, and there's a secular-sacred divide. When we fast and give time and finances to our family the poor, we are protesting against independent, selfish living and the lie that we are more valuable individually than the collective whole. When we partake of Communion, which is the one act Jesus asked us to do until his return—and live the Eucharist life—we protest against all wars and unjust suffering. We dethrone the kingdom of "self" as we invite others to come home to the new world that is already here in the risen Christ!

Your Story

"Look, I am coming soon! My reward is with me, and I will give to each person according to what they have done" (Rev. 22:12). No one knows when the divine trumpet will sound, so the Psalmist says, "Therefore let all the faithful pray to you while you may be found…" (Psalm 32:6). The following questions and exercises will help spiritually prepare you for the times that are to come, as you begin to make space to re-wild the state of your heart.

1. "Be self-controlled and alert. Your enemy the devil prowls around like a roaring lion looking for someone to devour" (1 Peter 5:8). In what areas of your life has the enemy been consistently pursuing you? Journal your realizations and where you lack self-discipline and mindfulness. What determinations are you going to make *now?* Share the results with a believing friend.

2. To re-wild our spirituality we seek God in the places where He often hides: the poor, the stranger, the widow, the unfamiliar, the soil of the earth and high hard places of land and sea. Sometimes these people and places are just around the corner from where we live. Commit to seek and find God in a place where you typically don't look for Him, where you are not in control. He is waiting for you

there.

3.What acts of protest can you adapt to usher in the new world, the Kingdom of God? Your acts of protest might be urban gardening, pursuing sustainable living, giving of your time and resources on behalf of the poor or issues of injustice.

Notes

"Attentive ears can hear the ancient whisper, reminding us that another world is possible."—Shane Claiborne [78]

Conclusion

Charlie's corner still looks vacant since he died over forty years ago. That corner, where our favorite policeman stood, was our ultimate safe place when we walked to school from my childhood home in Endicott, New York. Some afternoons, a little gang of school bullies would chase Gene and me up through the maze of streets. But we knew once we were close to Charlie's powerful presence on his corner, our terror-ridden sweat-bullets would evaporate. All would be well. We were safe with him, but we knew he also liked us. Once we stepped into the comfort of his shadow, Charlie gave us a quick wink, which made us feel older, wiser, and as if we were participants in a secret that no one else knew.

Then, he'd stuff a fistful of bazooka gum into the palm of our hands.

On busy afternoons, no matter how many kids were stacked on that street corner, Charlie always found us. Then he'd blow his whistle, and we'd stand to attention before we stepped onto the crosswalk.

Charlie probably never knew what he meant to us. His presence on that street corner provided a comforting assurance that we were loved by a stranger in this world, not just by family and friends. Upon seeing his rough but Santa-like face at the end of the school day, we could relax. Once we got to him, we knew we were almost home.

As a child I sensed the presence of God in my life through the wonder of all that was around me. At that time, He seemed like a loving stranger— too big and magnificent to be known. On days I thought He wasn't too busy, I'd imagine Him looking at me, giving me a joyful wink.

In some sense, Charlie prepared me to understand God. And God prepared me to be seen by Jesus.

In 2011, while leading Axiom Monastic Community in New Haven, Connecticut, I felt it was time to return home to visit my mother. I heard that her mental state was declining more quickly than Dad had anticipated. She was only 70 years old. Her life seemed to become suddenly fragile. My own sons had moved out of the home to start lives of their own. Axiom was now in a season where it didn't need my presence in New Haven. *What a joy,* I thought, *to help Dad with Mom, and to have unhurried time with them between my mission and teaching trips.* I had a five-month block of time where I could make their home my home base.

I arrived in Freeland, Washington, in the beginning of December. Dad and Mom were living there, and Dad worked part time for a ministry and with his heating and air conditioning business. While he worked in the morning hours, tool pouch on his hip, I helped care for Mom.

They couldn't have been more overjoyed to have me stay with them during the holiday season. On my first morning Mom said, "I'm so glad you are here, Jeff, to be with me. You are here to help me again."

"Again?" I asked.

"You've been my spiritual mentor for so long. But while you're here, what can I do for you? I don't cook anymore. Your father has been doing a good job at that. He's such a good man. He's been taking care of me."

"Well, Mom, there is one thing you can try to do," I suggested, pausing.

"O good," she replied as she looked at me with anticipation.

"I know I'm very late in finding the right woman to marry, but I still think she's out there somewhere. Maybe you can try to keep your memory till I find her?"

"Oh yes," she said. "I will try very hard."

"Remember, I've always wanted to take you and Dad to Italy, so after I get married you can come for the last part of our honeymoon there. How does that sound?"

"Very good," she said. "I don't want to miss that!"

One of my greatest joys during those five months was watching Mom become so child-like. I hadn't seen her that way since our old family camping trips. She would make fun of her short-term memory loss and her physical ailments, never with anger or bitterness, only occasional sadness. One day I caught her looking in the mirror as she slowly touched the many red marks on her face from scratching herself over and over again. One of her fingers paused on one of them and she said softly, "I used to think I was kind of pretty."

Just then Dad's voice came booming up the staircase, "Hey, Beautiful, come down here and watch the sun setting on the Olympic Mountains with me!"

She immediately dropped her hand and happily left her reflection to follow the love of her life.

I'll never forget the look on her face in that moment, the look of someone who has been uniquely adored and cherished by one man for over fifty years. What God couldn't give Mom in the flesh he did through my father, though she found it difficult to accept that love.

In the mornings I didn't have to be creative in how to entertain Mom. Her short-term memory was so bad she couldn't remember that I had just finished playing "I Dreamed and Dream," for her. She was equally impacted by it every morning. She'd say, "Doesn't that just grip your heart? How beautiful!" I thought, *Mom has become a true contemplative: she lives joyfully in the present moment every day and experiences life as if it's happening to her for the first time.*

Through dementia, Mom lost her self-conscious affect. She was no longer reluctant to inhabit a stranger's personal space. When she saw a baby in a restaurant she would greet the little one and compliment the parents. If we passed a friendly dog, she paused and acknowledged it. She was at peace with herself and the environment around her. To my amazement and joy her years of stress had finally come to an end.

Mom's long-term memory was still very much intact but without her usual filter. One afternoon as she sat next to me on the living room couch, she began to talk about the years she had been sexually abused, starting at five years old. She spoke of it so naturally that her tone was very matter of fact. When she had finished telling me the story, I placed my hand on hers and prayed.

I had prayed for many hurt and wounded people around the world through my ministry, but now I was finally able to pray for my own mom.

With the removal of Mom's stresses, the old Christmas magic that I hadn't seen her experience in years hung in the air with the scent of pine needles and nutmeg from her homemade eggnog. The difference now was that Dad was making the Christmas cookies while Mom and I frosted them. While I spread icing on one gingerbread man, Mom picked up a See's candy and put frosting on it, not realizing the difference. I gently guided her hand back to the cookies and was reminded of Brennan Manning's words, "God has ordained our latter days of our lives to look shockingly like that of our earliest; as dependent children."[79] His words particularly rang true when I was on my morning walk and Mom had secretly eaten all the rocky road ice cream out of the freezer and then acted as if she had no idea how it had disappeared. I smile at this memory now.

Christmas shopping for Mom was easy in the Bavarian-looking village of Leavenworth, Washington. We arrived a week before the holidays, and the charming little town was covered in snow and strung with thousands of soft green and red festive lights. We meandered from one shop to another. Mom had always loved to do that. We were winter figurines plodding across a Norman Rockwell Christmas postcard. It was idyllic.

In one store, Dad and I had Mom try on a few outfits which had caught her attention. "This angora sweater is so beautiful and soft," she said as she slowly ran her fingers over its sleeve. "I know it's too expensive," she said.

We bought the sweater even though she was there, knowing that it would still be a big surprise for her the following week. I remember her shock on Christmas morning, "I can't believe you found such a beautiful sweater that fits me perfectly! How did you do it?"

I wanted that holiday season to last forever.

All of us Pratt kids remember the moment Mom, for the first time, forgot that one of us was her own child. It had happened the week my brother Tim's two daughters were getting married. When Reid walked into the living room where all of us were gathered, Mom said, "Excuse me, who are you again?" We all laughed riotously, including Mom.

We realized that as time progressed Mom would only remember those with whom she had experienced a recent emotional connection. These connections helped plant you in her memory. Just showing up and quickly leaving were no guarantee. And as this realization dawned on us, a couple of us brothers made it a game. Which of us kids could be remembered the longest?

I look back on that time and reflect: what if the Ancient of Days only remembered those who were currently present with Him, in spirit, heart, and mind? What if we lived to be remembered?

A Homeward Call

One Wednesday night Dad and Mom had joined me for our Axiom practice of the weekly Eucharist. We had a beautiful time looking over our lives and remembering some of our greatest blessings. We reflected on our beginning years in Endicott, New York, our dear relatives, and all we had learned through being part of the Mormon Church.

"God has used everything," Dad said, "to draw us to Himself." Then we started talking about my siblings, and we prayed for each one. We prayed for Reid and Diana, and their kids, Kelton and Olivia, that someday they would be able to fulfill their dreams to Pastor (which they are doing now). We prayed for Gene, who had chosen life on the road, camping in various locations and enjoying the beauty of creation. I prayed, "May Gene sense Your presence in every place he resides."

"Don't forget Hopie and Kaitlyn," Mom interjected, who are Lee and Stephanie's children in Australia. She had visited them with Dad earlier in the year.

Then we thought of all the lives Tim and Becky's Orphan Relief and Rescue ministry was reaching in Liberia and Benin! We prayed for their orphanages and their safe houses, their children and grandchildren. We finished by praying for Steve in his beautiful adobe home in Santa Fe, and for Nicole and her wonderful three kids in Maryland.

April 2012, arrived too quickly. It was my time to head back to Connecticut to lead our spring retreats, and then to Europe for our summer pilgrimages. My time with Dad and Mom was coming to an end. Nicole had arrived to help. She would be followed by others. I'll never forget our last dinner at the El Corral, where I thoroughly enjoyed my favorite Acapulco Burrito, stuffed with crab meat. (You know my fond memories of crab!) At the end of the meal, Mom looked at me and said with sadness. "Jeff, you can't leave. Do you really have to go? Are you going to be okay?"

She paused and stared at me with those sad eyes. "I feel like we're deserting you," she continued. "Do you need money or anything? Are we sending you out into the world alone?" I could hardly swallow. I felt a burning sensation in my throat as I strained to contain the emotions that her statements so quickly evoked. In a wonderful way I felt like I was that young man back in Vancouver leaving home for the first time.

A couple of days earlier Mom had packed her things. "I'm going home as well," she told me. My parents were on Whidbey Island for two years to work, but they would be returning to the first home they had owned in east Texas in the upcoming summer. Occasionally Mom would get her timing mixed up and would want to suddenly return there.

"Just a couple months from now Mom," I would say to her. She'd reply with a scowl of disappointment as she began to unpack her things again. After unpacking, she'd relax and say with a nostalgic look in her eyes "almost home."

For the next six months, my travels took me on a glorious romp around some of my favorite parts of the world. I lived out James 1:27, a verse that has captured my contemplative activism: "Religion that God our Father accepts as pure and faultless is this: to look after orphans and widows in their distress and to keep oneself from being polluted by the world." I took pilgrimage to India and Nepal. We practiced the first emphasis of James 1:27 while caring for orphans and widows in Pune, India. This was followed by a glorious hike near the roof of the world in Nepal, as we talked about what it meant to remain unpolluted by the world.

Throughout my travels I received updates from Dad of Mom's progressive decline in east Texas. She had started to eat and talk less, and she was unhappy to be back in Texas. It broke Dad's heart. One day she said in anguish, "I'm lonely. I want to go home."

Home to Mom was no longer a place. Likely, it meant having us, her children, around her again.

Doctors began saying that Mom had six months to live, but they dropped it down to two months. After Mom stopped communicating, her decline was rapid. The family felt it best for her to be transported to Steve's larger house in Santa Fe, New Mexico.

One early Wednesday morning, while teaching a series called "The Spiritual Pathways," in Belize, I received a knock on the door. It was one of my friends, Allysen George. She had a very sober yet compassionate expression on her face as she handed a phone to me and said, "It's your father." Knowing Mom's condition, I quickly pulled the receiver close to my ear.

"My son, your mother stopped eating a couple of days ago and right now her breathing is very slight," he said. "I don't know if she's getting ready to pass or not. If you get a quick flight to Santa Fe, maybe you can make it before she does."

"What should I do," I asked?

"I don't know son," he replied.

I had hardly ever heard Dad say the words: *I don't know,* especially in a difficult situation. After a moment of tense frustration, I thought, *if there's anything I've learned in my life it is this: God is right here, right now, and He responds to His children.*

I paused on the phone and whispered, "Father, are you coming for Mom? Is her time now?" I instantly knew the answer.

"Turn on the speaker phone, Dad," I said.

Neither of us knew if she was conscience or not, but that didn't seem to matter.

I began to thank Mom for so much, with a depth of emotion I had never shown her before. It culminated when I said to her, "Most of all, Mom, I want to thank you for giving me Jesus. This half-deaf-rocker-runner would never have known true love and the joy of taking God's healing to the nations, if it wasn't for you. Also, when you see your mom, the grandmother I never knew, let her know of all that her sacrifice has won for the Kingdom of our God."

At that moment I felt a hesitation in Mom's spirit. Reluctance, as if she didn't feel worthy of heaven, so I said, "It's okay for you to go Mom. God is waiting for you—you are His desire. Goodbye Mom."

Within fifteen minutes she fell into the loving arms of our God.

As I slowly sat down on the bed in my cabana, my spirit sank into a warm ocean of peace. I imagined Dad at that moment, alone. Left by his Philly, the one he had lived for and had served for as long as I could remember. I imagined him leaning his head against hers one last time, as he whispered his old familiar words, "I will love you forever and a day."

We all gathered in Santa Fe for Mom's Memorial. Dad gave each
of us a poem Mom had written about us at some point in our lives.
Her prophetic nature shone brightly through the words she had written
about me when I was 15 years old.

> I saw a bird fly through the sky
> On wings of burnished gold
> He glided to a rambling bush
> And sang a song so bold.
>
> He spoke of beauty on the wing
> Of places beyond the sea
> He dropped a secret in my heart,
> A longing to be free.
>
> Free to fly among the flock
> To see the world so wide
> To see beyond the works of men
> And far beyond the sky.

In the emotional turbulence of my teen years, Mom had seen me
as God dreamed me into being. And by God's grace, He's still
dreaming me into being.

Over the years I have had seasons of great satisfaction as well as
times of deep need. Both have been necessary companions on my
spiritual journey. There are questions I've had about this good life.
Many things I don't understand. A deeply respected teacher, Tom
Bloomer, said, "When we pray, we are trusting God; when He doesn't
answer, He is trusting us to keep on trusting Him, and not to lose our
hope."

I attempt to live life's questions with a nurtured hope.

If my bride never comes, or if I'm too blind to see her, I know that God is always coming. When I grow weary as I run away from the bullies of this present age, those who conspire against the interior life, I step into the safety of His shadow. It is there I pause and catch His wink, which often turns into a gaze. There, I rest in wonder and know that I am almost home.

An Awakened Life

On a cold winter's night, during my pre-adoptive year with my sons, Patrick and I were sitting on our living room couch watching TV. Being of Irish descent, Patrick has the boldest orange-red hair you've ever seen, along with bright blue eyes, freckles everywhere, and skin that is so white he gets a sunburn when he reaches into the microwave!

After joking during a commercial, Pat got quiet and leaned against my chest. About 20 minutes later, he whispered, "Dad where are you going? Don't you love me anymore? If you go this time, I don't think I'm going to make it."

I had no idea why he would say such a thing. I wasn't planning to go away.

Startled at hearing these words, I glanced down at his face and saw that he had fallen asleep. The words coming out of his mouth were words from a fractured heart and past hurts of abandonment.

With an unrestrained joy, as his new father, I gently shook his little shoulders and whispered into his ear, "Patrick, my son, wake up, and see where you are."

His bright blue eyes opened wide. Relief and joy flooded his face as he saw that he was held, loved, and couldn't be closer to me than he already was.

I am convinced that the Father's greatest joy is to help us fulfill His Son's last command to His disciples in the Garden of Gethsemane, which is, "Wake Up!" When His followers heard this commission to be alert and to wait with Jesus, they found it a task impossible to do. In this present age, we face a similar struggle. Spiritual Alzheimer's has lulled us into forgetting our true identity and the words of the inner music of our belovedness to God—what C.S. Lewis described as "the music that resembles an earlier music that men are born remembering."[80] Through an on-going journey with the spiritual practices we will *wake up* to the baffling reality that the Trinity has made their home in us, beckoning us to participate with them in their scandalous redemptive dreams for the world. May you find the below resources helpful towards this end.

Applying a Practice to a Personal Need

Practices are relational acts where we respond to, and cultivate intimacy with God and others. The following are some practices you can employ for various needs:

Lack of energy- body care (exercise/diet), the Jesus Prayer

The plague of questions and unbelief- bible study, scripture praying, worship

Isolation/loneliness- spiritual companionship, acts of service

Sleeplessness- the prayer of examen, body care

Distracted mind- contemplative prayer, biblical meditation

Cleansing from guilt and pride– confession, scripture reading, fasting

Intimacy needs- prayer in creation, worship, communion/ the Eucharist

Depression/sadness- thanksgiving/worship, acts of service, encourage others

Narcissistic spirituality (A me-centered life)- giving, intercession, acts of service

Boredom- acts of service, pilgrimage

The Prayer of Examen

"Examine yourself to see whether you are in the faith: test yourselves. Do you not realize that Christ Jesus is in you, unless of course you fail the test." 2 Cor. 13:5

The Examen is a method of reviewing your day in the presence of God. It's actually an attitude more than a method, a time set aside for thankful reflection on where God is in your everyday life. It has five steps and it usually takes 15 to 20 minutes per day. The steps are as follows:

1. Be aware of God's presence. Look back on the events of the day in the company of the Holy Spirit. Ask God for clarity and understanding.

2. Review the day with gratitude. Note the day's joys, gifts and delights. Take joy in the seemingly small pleasures.

3. Pay attention to the movements of your emotions. Discern where you loved well and where you held back. What is God showing you?

4. Choose one feature of the day and pray for it. Allow the prayers to rise spontaneously from your heart, whether intercessory prayers, prayers of praise, or prayers of repentance or gratitude.

5. Look towards tomorrow. Turn your thoughts and feelings about tomorrow into prayers of hope, and anticipation of your partnership with God. [81]

The Path of Ascent and Descent

"Let's remind ourselves that contemplative activism combines two ideas, the first one being the essential, yet often lost art of drawing aside with God for prayer and learning how to find Him in every aspect of life. Contemplative experience provides a door to discovering so much more about ourselves, each other, and God and His ways.

However there is a danger. Having ascended the heights through contemplation, we may not want to return and make our descent back into the streets of chaos within which we are called to carry out the mission of God. Secondly, therefore, we seek to live out prayer by rolling up our sleeves and serving the needs of the surrounding community. The contemplative activist develops the rhythm of ascent and descent in living the Spirit-filled life." – Dr. Micha Jazz [82]

Recommended readings for aspiring contemplative activists, and other resources can be found at our Axiom Monastic Community website: www.christouraxiom.com

JEFF PRATT is an ordained, international speaker, and writer, who is founder and spiritual director of Axiom Monastic Community, a global network of contemplative activists and missional communities. He treasures time with his adopted sons in New Haven, Connecticut— between lion walks in Zimbabwe— and immersing himself in the needs and wonders of children, the poor, and creation. He connects with old friends and new at:

jeff-pratt.com

Acknowledgements

This book has emerged because of those who have witnessed the movements of God in my life, from my early years as a Mormon, to my journey with Jesus, and into the nations. First, I want to thank my sister-in-law, Rebecca Pratt, for hounding me until I wrote my story. This book would not exist if it weren't for her tenacious belief in me and my message. I want to thank Lori Janke for her initial editing skills. Michael Cotton took on the reigns after Lori, and what can I say but: *you are an invaluable friend, editor, and fellow pilgrim in this life.* After Michael's assistance I felt a need to condense my manuscript, and undergo a final edit by someone who didn't know me. Through divine guidance, and John Ray, I was led into the skillful hands of a gifted writer and newfound friend, Seth Haines: *thank you for your assistance, and your kindred spirit for all things monastic.*

Ron Adair, my artist, did an exceptional job capturing each chapter theme, and his partnership on this project far exceeded my expectations.

I must mention my extreme gratitude for those who helped facilitate the final sprint of this race: Marilyn Murray who crafted the stand-out book cover, and Jen Cherrington (Jennifer rae design): *your design skills, and encouragement have helped make this project a home run*!

I have lived the pilgrim's life on the road for almost five years now and began this project during that time. I want to express my thanks to all the gracious folks who hosted me, giving me space to process and write, with the occasional respite of a movie and good food. Special thanks to Edith and Jason Benjamin for opening their home to this vagabond for longer than we had anticipated— *Jason, who would of thought, meeting you at an altar call in Mt. View Christian Center over thirty years ago, we'd still be friends, learning the journey of surrender as much now, as we did then. Edith you are more than you know, the backbone to so much.* Thanks to my brother in Santa Fe, Steve: *even after the hardest days of writing, experiencing your cooking, accompanied by "The Good Wife," made every visit a memorable experience. It's been fun becoming friends again.*

This section would be incomplete without mentioning Brenda Lewis, and Jeremy and Ricci Harke who carry so well the treasures of home and friendship. Other special homes abroad included my dear Catalina friends and activists, Scott and Darlene Schmeckpeper, my British co-conspirator Johnny Sertin, and his beloved family and community, and my Pacific Northwest haven, Steve and Ronelle Tibbits. All are such gifts to me.

I wrote the last chapter and conclusion of my book where my life began in Endicott, upstate New York. Aunt Donna and Uncle Dale Burrell, there couldn't have been a better place to finish my memoir.

Also, I want to personally thank the following people for their contributions to my inspiration and knowledge and other help in creating this book: Linda Apple, Derek Schoenhoff (what a gift you've been!), Mrs. Elsie Schoenff, Kathelyze Trejo, Joshua and Carrie Smith, Rob and Christel Morris, Hana Kim, Michelle Priestly, Tammie Hull, Jerry Johnson, Kathleen and Henry Hess, Dave and Kathy Mc-Cracken, Shelley Hepler, Micha and Jayne Jazz, and my CPC Staten Island, and Bronx family —even you Vinny.

I want to thank Roger and Deb Andruss, and our Axiom Communities, for all your prayers, and giving me the time to put my life into written words. And lastly, TinaFara Rusike, and my extended African family in Zimbabwe— know that while this work is being published I'll be missing you all desperately.

Axiom's
Pilgrimages & Retreats

Consider joining us on an Axiom pilgrimage
or retreat to one of the following locations:

Re-Wilding Wilderness Retreat • Montana

Celtic Ireland • Cong

St. Francis's • Assisi, Italy

" **There is something significant in making a journey.** Granted, all the things we encountered on the retreat are things that may be found in other places. But when combined with the journey of a pilgrimage, they take on a defined brightness and are able to penetrate deeper into the soul "

-Josanna Justine

Are Mormons Christians?

I explore this question and other relevant topics at:

jeff-pratt.com

Endnotes

Intro

1 Chronicles 16:11, 2 Chronicles 7:14, Psalm 27:8, Psalm 105:4.

2 Frederick Buechner, *Telling Secrets* (New York: HarperCollins Publishers, 1991).

Chapter 1

3 Stan Miller and Sharon Miller, *Especially for Mormons,* Vol. 1 (Provo: Kellirae Arts, 1997), 54.

4 Dallas Willard, "Live Life to The Full," *Christian Herald,* April 14, 2001.

5 The name of the location of this women's care home for prostitutes has been changed to protect her identity and ministry.

6 Richard Rohr, *Everything Belongs: The Gift of Contemplative Prayer* (New York: The Crossroad Publishing Company, 1999), 31.

7 Marion A. Habig, ed., *St. Francis of Assisi: Omnibus of Sources* (Chicago: Franciscan Herald Press, 1973), 74.

8 Fr. Pedro Arrupe, SJ, *Finding God in All Places: A Marquette Prayer Book* (Milwaukee: Marquette University Press, 2009), 100.

Chapter 2

9 Frederick Buechner, *Wishful Thinking: A Seeker's ABC* (New York: Harper One, 1973).

10 St. John of the Cross, Kieran Kavanaugh, trans., Otilio Rodriguez, trans., *The Collected Works of St. John of the Cross* (Washington, D.C., ICS Publications, 1979).

11 These first three lines are a portion of Esther de Wall's beautiful prayer to the Trinity found in *The Celtic Way of Prayer: the Recovery of the Religious Imagination* (New York: Doubleday 1997), 43.

Chapter 3

12 To protect the identity of the mentioned couple, I have changed their names here.

13 Peter Scazzero, *Emotionally Healthy Spirituality* (Grand Rapids: Zondervan, 2006), 33.

14 Robert Bly, *Iron John: A Book About Men* (Boston: Da Capo Press, 1990).

Chapter 4

15 Thomas Merton, *New Seeds of Contemplation* (New York: New Directions Paperbook, 1961).

16 Helen Steiner Rice, *The Story of the Christmas Guest* (Tarrytown: F.H. Revell Co., 1972).

17 Father Ron Rolheiser, "The Christian Task is to Stand at The Foot of the Cross," *The Catholic Star Herald*, accessed August 13, 2016, http://catholicstarherald.org/the-christian-task-is-to-stand-at-the-foot-of-the-cross.

18 Craig Greenfield, *All about God, his mission and his world,* accessed September 26, 2016, http://www.craiggreenfield.com/blog/2015/3/4/stop-calling-it-short-term-missions.

19 Dr. Micha Jazz is a dear friend, writer, broadcaster, storyteller, and Axiom advisor. For more information on his retreats, visit: stcuthbertsoratory.com. I also recommend to you his popular devotional book, *Be Still & Know,* a reflection of every day of the year, which is available from: http://www.premier.org.uk/Shop/Be-Still-Know.

20 A phrase commonly used by mystics throughout the centuries.

Chapter 5

21 Corrie Ten Boom, *The Hiding Place* (Grand Rapids: Chosen Books, 1971), 240.

22 Fr. Thomas Keating, *The Method of Centering Prayer, The Prayer of Consent* (Contemplative Outreach LTD Pamphlet, 2006).

23 *See* Martin Laird, *Into the Silent Land* (Oxford: Oxford University Press 2006), 70-80.

24 Ibid., 106.

Chapter 6

25 Erich Przywara, ed., *An Austine Synthesis* (Eugene: Wipf and Stock Publishers, 2014).

26 Oswald Chambers, *My Utmost For His Highest* (New York: Dodd,

Mead & Company, Inc. 1935).

27 *See* Isaiah 6:1-8.

28 *See* Brennan Manning, *Abba's Child: The Cry of The Heart For Intimate Belonging* (Colorado Springs: NavPress, 1994).

29 Richard Foster, *Prayer: Finding The Heart's True Home* (New York: HarperSanFrancisco, 1992).

30 Neal Donald Welsch, "*Something Old, Something New,*" accessed September 28, 2016, http://soul-essence.com/2011/101.

31 Richard Foster, *Celebration of The Disciplines: The Path to Spiritual Growth* (New York: HarperSanfrancisco, 1978).

Chapter 7

32 Keith Green, "Asleep in the Light," lyrics copyrighted by Warner/Chapell Music, Inc.

Chapter 9

33 Pico Iyer, "Where is Your Home," TedGlobal, filmed June, 2013.

34 Shane Claiborne, *The Irresistible Revolution: Living as an Ordinary Radical* (Grand Rapids: Zondervan, 2006), 65.

35 Kevin Halloren, "The 15 Best James Hudson Taylor Quotes," *Leadership Resources*, accessed September 28, 2016, http://www.leadershipresources.org/the-15-best-james-hudson-taylor-quotes.

36 Richard Rohr, "Silence as an Alternative Consciousness," *Richard Rohr's Daily Meditation* (Center for Action and Contemplation, Tuesday, Dec. 23, 2014).

37 Nicki Verploegen Vandergrift, *Meditation with Merton:A Collage of Scripture Quotes, Original Prayers, and Merton's Own Words,* (Eugene: Wipf and Stock Publishers, 1993), 87.

38 *See* Richard Rohr, *Eager to Love: The Alternative Way of Francis of Assisi* (Cincinnati: Franciscan Media, 2014), 42.

Chapter 10

39 Bill Murphy, Jr., "87 Inspiring Quotes For Martin Luther King's 87th Birthday," *Inc.com*, last accessed September 28, 2016, http://www.inc.com/bill-murphy-jr/87-inspiring-quotes-for-martin-luther-king-87th-birthday.html.

40 W. Lorett, "Social Political Morality 6," *Oxford Dictionary of Proverbs* (Oxford: Oxford University Press, 1982), 293.

Chapter 11

41 C.S. Lewis wrote this in a correspondence to Reverend Peter Bide on April 29th, 1959, said letter which is collected in Letters of C.S. Lewis, edited by Warnie Lewis and published in 1966. The correspondence is not found in the most recent publications of the collected letters of Lewis.

42 The Old Testament books of Daniel and Esther are concerned exclusively with the events that occurred in the exile.

43 Amy Carmichael, "Royal Purposes," *Scarred Battle* (Richmond: Harvey Christian Publishers, 1963).

44 William McNamara as quoted by Walter J. Burghandt, "Contemplation: A Long Loving Look at The Real," Church, No. 5 (1989), 14-17.

Chapter 12

45 *See* Brennan Manning, *Abba's Child: The Cry of The Heart For Intimate Belonging* (Colorado Springs: NavPress, 1994).

Chapter 13

46 St. John of the Cross, Kieran Kavanaugh, trans., Otilio Rodriguez, trans., *The Collected Works of St. John of the Cross* (Washington, D.C., ICS Publications, 1979).

Chapter 14

47 Curt Thompson, M.D., *Anatomy of the Soul: Surprising Connections Between Neuroscience and Spiritual Practices That Can Transform Your Life and Relationships* (Carol Stream: Tyndale Momentum, 2010).

48 Rev. Janet Robertson Duggins, "*Being the Beloved Community,*" from the Portage, Michigan Westminster Presbyterian Church website, last accessed September 28, 2016, https://www.google.com/#q=Rev.+-Janet+Robertson+Duggins+article%2C+%22Being+the+Beloved+Community.

49 *See* Richard Rohr, *Eager to Love: The Alternative Way of Francis of Assisi* (Cincinnati: Franciscan Media, 2014), 106.

50 Watchman Nee, *The Normal Christian Life* (Bombay, India: Gospel Literature Service, 1957).

51 C.S. Lewis, *Till We Have Faces: A Myth Retold* (London: Geoffrey Bless, 1956).

52 J.R.R. Tolkein, *The Fellowship of the Ring: Being the First Part of The Lord of the Rings* (London: George Allen & Unwin, 1954).

53 This quote is attributed to Mother Teresa. *See http://www.goodreads.com/quotes/23380-if-we-have-no-peace-it-is-because-we-have*, accessed on October 2, 2016.

54 This phrase comes from Dr. Micha Jazz. *See* endnote #19.

Chapter 15

55 Parker Palmer, "Sitting in Circles," *Beliefnet*, accessed September 28, 2016, www.beliefnet.com/inspiration/2004/10/sitting-in-circles.aspx.

56 Ronald Rolheiser, *Our One Great Act of Fidelity: Waiting for Christ in the Eucharist* (New York: Image, 2011), 95.

57 Ibid.

58 This list of scriptures can be found in Richard Foster's classic, *Celebration of Discipline: The Path to Spiritual Growth* (New York: HarperSanFrancisco, 1978), 97.

59 Axiom is in partnership with Steve Schallert and his team that leads YWAM's "A Life Together" Discipleship Training School. Steve's worship CD "*Songs of Sorrow, Songs of Hope,*" has also been a great blessing to our Axiom Monastic Communities. You can find it at https://steveschallert.bandcamp.com/album/songs-of-sorrow-songs-of-hope.

60 Fr. Michael Lapsley, SSM, *Redeeming the Past* (New York: Orbis Books, 2012).

61 Ronald Rolheiser, *Our One Great Act of Fidelity: Waiting for Christ in the Eucharist* (New York: Image, 2011), 110-11.

62 Frederick Buechner, *Listening to Your Life: Daily Meditations With Frederick Buechner* (New York: HarperSanFransico, 1992), 186.

63 St. John of the Cross, Kieran Kavanaugh, trans., Otilio Rodriguez, trans., *The Collected Works of St. John of the Cross* (Washington, D.C., ICS Publications, 1979).

64 Ibid., 95.

65 Anthony De Mello, *Wellsprings: A Book of Spiritual Exercises* (New York: Doubleday, 1984), 120 – 21.

Chaper 16

66 Joseph Smith, *The Pearl of Great Price, History of Joseph Smith* (Full HTML Text, official LDS Church edition, lds.org) 18 - 20.

67 Manafo, J. & Yoder, J.H. *And We Will Become a Happy Ending* (Sarnia, ON: Storyboard Solutions, 2012), 27.

68 Acts 17:28.

69 An example of The Prayer of Examen is in the appendix.

70 Pete Askew, *New Monasticism as Fresh Expression of Church – Pilgrimage* (Canterbury: Canterbury Press, 2010), 101.

71 Lewis B. Smedes, *Standing on the Promises*. (Washville: Thomas Nelson, 1998.)

72 *See* Richard Rohr, "Gospel Call for Compassionate Action" found in CAC Foundation Set (CAC:2007) CD, MP3 download.

Chapter 17

73 Pete Askew's excellent chapter on pilgrimage in *New Monasticism as Fresh Expression of Church* (CanterburyPress, 2010) has helped frame my experience and language during my years of walking the pilgrim's way.

74 *See* Pete Askew, *New Monasticism as Fresh Expression of Church* (Canterbury: CanterburyPress, 2010), 98.

75 Ian Morgan Cron, *Chasing Francis: A Pilgrims Tale,* (Grand Rapids: Zondervann, 2006).

76 Reverend Johnny Sertin is Cofounder and trustee of The Paradise Cooperative in south London, an urban *farm to fork* community venture curating "space to grow." Johnny and his community are part of our Axiom network.

77 C.S. Lewis, *Mere Christianity* (1952; HarperCollins: 2001) 45-46.

78 Shane Claiborne, *The Irresistible Revolution: Living as an Ordinary Radical* (Grand Rapids: Zondervan, 2006), 65.

Conclusion

79 Brennan Manning, John Blase, *All is Grace: A Ragamuffin Memoir* (Colorado Springs: David C. Cook, 2011).

Appendix

80 C.S. Lewis, "*Vowels and Sirens,*" as quoted by Ken Gire, *The Divine Embrace* (Carol Stream: Tyndale House Publishers, Inc., 2003), 82.

81 More information about the daily examen may be found by visiting http://www.ignatianspirituality.com/ignatian-prayer/the-examen/how-can-i-pray.

82 *See* to endnote #19.